D. Patrick Zimmerman, PsyD

The Forsaken Child:
Essays on Group Care
and Individual Therapy

The Forsaken Child: Essays on Group Care and Individual Therapy has been co-published simultaneously as *Residential Treatment for Children & Youth,* Volume 18, Number 2 2000.

*Pre-publication
REVIEWS,
COMMENTARIES,
EVALUATIONS . . .*

"**A** MUST READ for anyone concerned about the quality of care of disturbed children and youth. Zimmerman is truly the 'great chronicler' and the 'keeper of the flame' of quality group care."

Robert B. Bloom, PhD
*Executive Director,
Jewish Children's Bureau,
Chicago, Illinois*

The Forsaken Child:
Essays on Group Care
and Individual Therapy

The Forsaken Child: Essays on Group Care and Individual Therapy has been co-published simultaneously as *Residential Treatment for Children & Youth*, Volume 18, Number 2 2000.

The *Residential Treatment for Children & Youth* Monographic "Separates"

Below is a list of "separates," which in serials librarianship means a special issue simultaneously published as a special journal issue or double-issue *and* as a "separate" hardbound monograph. (This is a format which we also call a "DocuSerial.")

"Separates" are published because specialized libraries or professionals may wish to purchase a specific thematic issue by itself in a format which can be separately cataloged and shelved, as opposed to purchasing the journal on an on-going basis. Faculty members may also more easily consider a "separate" for classroom adoption.

"Separates" are carefully classified separately with the major book jobbers so that the journal tie-in can be noted on new book order slips to avoid duplicate purchasing.

You may wish to visit Haworth's website at . . .

http://www.HaworthPress.com

. . . to search our online catalog for complete tables of contents of these separates and related publications.

You may also call 1-800-HAWORTH (outside US/Canada: 607-722-5857), or Fax: 1-800-895-0582 (outside US/Canada: 607-771-0012), or e-mail at:

getinfo@haworthpressinc.com

The Forsaken Child: Essays on Group Care and Individual Therapy, by D. Patrick Zimmerman, PsyD (Vol. 18, No. 2, 2000). *"A MUST READ for anyone concerned about the quality of care of disturbed children and youth. Zimmerman is truly the 'great chronicler' and the 'keeper of the flame' of quality group care." (Robert B. Bloom, PhD, Executive Director, Jewish Children's Bureau, Chicago, Illinois)*

Family-Centered Services in Residential Treatment: New Approaches for Group Care, edited by John Y. Powell, PhD (Vol. 17, No. 3, 2000). *"Offers suggestions and methods for incorporating parents and youths into successful treatment programs in temporary and long-term settings. This essential guide will help psychologists, therapists, and social workers unite theory and practice to create a family-oriented environment for troubled clients and provide effective services. Containing case studies, personal discoveries, and insights about the potentials and limitations of residential care, this reliable resource will help you develop improved services for youths with the help of their families using reevaluated techniques to meet individual needs."*

The New Board: Changing Issues, Roles and Relationships, edited by Nadia Ehrlich Finkelstein, MS, ACSW, and Raymond Schimmer, MAT (Vol. 16, No. 4, 1999). *This innovative book offers very specific, real life examples and informed recommendations for board management of nonprofit residential service agencies and explains why and how to consider redesigning your board form and practice. You will explore variations of board structures, managed care pressure, increased complexity of service, reduced board member availability, and relevant theoretical discussions complete with pertinent reports on the practice of boards in the nonprofit residential service field.*

Outcome Assessment in Residential Treatment, edited by Steven I. Pfeiffer, PhD (Vol. 13, No. 4, 1996). *"Presents a logical and systematic response, based on research, to the detractors of residential treatment centers." (Canada's Children (Child Welfare League of Canada))*

Residential Education as an Option for At-Risk Youth, edited by Jerome Beker, EdD, and Douglas Magnuson, MA (Vol. 13, No. 3, 1996). *"As a remarkable leap forward, as an approach to child welfare, it is required reading for professionals–from child care workers to administrators and planners–or for anyone in search of hope for children trapped in the bitter problems of a blighted and disordered existence . . . It is instructive, practical, and humanistic." (Howard Goldstein, DSW, Professor Emeritus, Case Western Reserve University; Author, The Home on Gorham Street)*

When Love Is Not Enough: The Management of Covert Dynamics in Organizations that Treat Children and Adolescents, edited by Donna Piazza, PhD (Vol. 13, No. 1, 1996). *"Addresses the difficult*

question of 'unconscious dynamics' within institutions which care for children and adolescents. The subject matter makes for fascinating reading, and anyone who has had experience of residential institutions for disturbed children will find themselves nodding in agreement throughout the book."
(Emotional and Behavioural Difficulties)

Applied Research in Residential Treatment, edited by Gordon Northrup, MD (Vol. 12, No. 1, 1995). *"The authors suggest appropriate topics for research projects, give practical suggestions on design, and provide example research reports." (Reference & Research Book News)*

Managing the Residential Treatment Center in Troubled Times, edited by Gordon Northrup, MD (Vol. 11, No. 4, 1994). *"A challenging manual for a challenging decade. . . .Takes the eminently sensible position that our failures are as worthy of analysis as our successes. This approach is both sobering and instructive." (Nancy Woodruff Ment, MSW, BCD, Associate Executive Director, Julia Dyckman Andrus Memorial, Yonkers, New York)*

The Management of Sexuality in Residential Treatment, edited by Gordon Northrup, MD (Vol. 11, No. 2, 1994). *"Must reading for residential treatment center administrators and all treatment personnel." (Irving N. Berlin, MD, Emeritus Professor, School of Medicine, University of New Mexico; Clinical Director, Child & Adolescent Services, Charter Hospital of Albuquerque and Medical Director, Namaste Residential Treatment Center)*

Sexual Abuse and Residential Treatment, edited by Wander de C. Braga, MD, and Raymond Schimmer (Vol. 11, No. 1, 1994). *"Ideas are presented for assisting victims in dealing with past abuse and protecting them from future abuse in the facility." (Coalition Commentary (Illinois Coalition Against Sexual Assault))*

Milieu Therapy: Significant Issues and Innovative Applications, edited by Jerome M. Goldsmith, EdD, and Jacquelyn Sanders, PhD (Vol. 10, No. 3, 1993). *This tribute to Bruno Bettelheim illuminates continuing efforts to further understanding of the caring process and its impact upon healing and repair measures for disturbed children in residential care.*

Severely Disturbed Youngsters and the Parental Alliance, edited by Jacquelyn Sanders, PhD, and Barry L. Childress, MD (Vol. 9, No. 4, 1992). *"Establishes the importance of a therapeutic alliance with the parents of severely disturbed young people to improve the success of counseling." (Public Welfare)*

Crisis Intervention in Residential Treatment: The Clinical Innovations of Fritz Redl, edited by William C. Morse, PhD (Vol. 8, No. 4, 1991). *"Valuable in helping us set directions for continuing Redl's courageous trail-blazing work." (Reading (A Journal of Reviews and Commentary in Mental Health))*

Adolescent Suicide: Recognition, Treatment and Prevention, edited by Barry Garfinkel, MD, and Gordon Northrup, MD (Vol. 7, No. 1, 1990). *"Distills highly relevant information about the identification and treatment of suicidal adolescents into a pithy volume which will be highly accessible by all mental health professionals." (Norman E. Alessi, MD, Director, Child Diagnostic and Research Unit, The University of Michigan Medical Center)*

Psychoanalytic Approaches to the Very Troubled Child: Therapeutic Practice Innovations in Residential and Educational Settings, edited by Jacquelyn Sanders, PhD, and Barry M. Childress, MD (Vol. 6, No. 4, 1989). *"I find myself wanting to re-read the book–which I recommend for every professional library shelf, especially for directors of programs dealing with the management of residentially located disturbed youth." (Journal of American Association of Psychiatric Administrators)*

The Forsaken Child:
Essays on Group Care
and Individual Therapy

D. Patrick Zimmerman, PsyD

The Forsaken Child: Essays on Group Care and Individual Therapy has been co-published simultaneously as *Residential Treatment for Children & Youth*, Volume 18, Number 2 2000.

The Haworth Press, Inc.
New York • London • Oxford

The Forsaken Child: Essays on Group Care and Individual Therapy has been co-published simultaneously as *Residential Treatment for Children & Youth* ™, Volume 18, Number 2 2000.

The development, preparation, and publication of this work has been undertaken with great care. However, the publisher, employees, editors, and agents of The Haworth Press and all imprints of The Haworth Press, Inc., including The Haworth Medical Press® and Pharmaceutical Products Press®, are not responsible for any errors contained herein or for consequences that may ensue from use of materials or information contained in this work. Opinions expressed by the author(s) are not necessarily those of The Haworth Press, Inc.

Cover design by Thomas J. Mayshock Jr.

Library of Congress Cataloging-in-Publication Data

Zimmerman, D. Patrick, Psy.D.
    The forsaken child: essays on group care and individual therapy/D. Patrick Zimmerman.
        p. cm.
    "Co-published simultaneously as Residential treatment for children & youth, volume 18, number 2 2000."
    Includes bibliographical references and index.
    ISBN 0-7890-1318-5 (alk. paper)–ISBN 0-7890-1319-3 (alk. paper)
    1. Child psychotherapy–Residential treatment. 2. Children–Institutional care. 3. Group homes for children. I. Residential treatment for children & youth. II. Title.

RJ504.5.Z55 2001
618.92′8914–dc21
                                                                        00-065349

Indexing, Abstracting & Website/Internet Coverage

This section provides you with a list of major indexing & abstracting services. That is to say, each service began covering this periodical during the year noted in the right column. Most Websites which are listed below have indicated that they will either post, disseminate, compile, archive, cite or alert their own Website users with research-based content from this work. (This list is as current as the copyright date of this publication.)

Abstracting, Website/Indexing Coverage . . . . Year When Coverage Began

- *Applied Social Sciences Index & Abstracts (ASSIA) (Online: ASSI via Data-Star) (CDRom: ASSIA Plus)* **1993**

- *BUBL Information Service, an Internet-based Information Service for the UK higher education community <URL: http://bubl.ac.uk/>* **1995**

- *Cambridge Scientific Abstracts (Risk Abstracts) <www.csa.com>* . . **1982**

- *Child Development Abstracts & Bibliography (in print and online)* . . . **1982**

- *CNPIEC Reference Guide: Chinese National Directory of Foreign Periodicals* **1995**

- *Criminal Justice Abstracts* **1982**

- *Exceptional Child Education Resources (ECER) (CD/ROM from SilverPlatter and hard copy)* **1982**

- *Family Studies Database (online and CD/ROM) <www.nisc.com>* . . . **1996**

- *FINDEX <www.publist.com>* **1999**

- *IBZ International Bibliography of Periodical Literature* **1996**

- *Index to Periodical Articles Related to Law* **1991**

- *International Bulletin of Bibliography on Education* **1992**

(continued)

*Special Bibliographic Notes related to special journal issues
(separates) and indexing/abstracting:*

- indexing/abstracting services in this list will also cover material in any "separate" that is co-published simultaneously with Haworth's special thematic journal issue or DocuSerial. Indexing/abstracting usually covers material at the article/chapter level.
- monographic co-editions are intended for either non-subscribers or libraries which intend to purchase a second copy for their circulating collections.
- monographic co-editions are reported to all jobbers/wholesalers/approval plans. The source journal is listed as the "series" to assist the prevention of duplicate purchasing in the same manner utilized for books-in-series.
- to facilitate user/access services all indexing/abstracting services are encouraged to utilize the co-indexing entry note indicated at the bottom of the first page of each article/chapter/contribution.
- this is intended to assist a library user of any reference tool (whether print, electronic, online, or CD-ROM) to locate the monographic version if the library has purchased this version but not a subscription to the source journal.
- individual articles/chapters in any Haworth publication are also available through the Haworth Document Delivery Service (HDDS).

The Forsaken Child: Essays on Group Care and Individual Therapy

CONTENTS

ABOUT THE AUTHOR

D. Patrick Zimmerman, PsyD, is Coordinator of Research, the Sonia Shankman Orthogenic School, Lecturer, the Department of Psychiatry, University of Chicago, and a member of the Senior Associate Core Faculty at the Illinois School of Professional Psychology/Chicago. He is a graduate of the Chicago Center for Psychoanalysis and has published articles on residential treatment, child psychotherapy, and psychoanalysis.

Foreword

Writing in a preface to his colleague August Aichhorn's (1925) report on psychoanalytic work with delinquent young people, *Wayward Youth*, Freud observed that: "None of the applications of psychoanalysis has excited so much interest and aroused so many hopes, and none, consequently, has attracted so many capable workers as its use in the theory and practice of education" (Freud, 1925/1960, p. 273). Freud's understanding of the important interplay of psychoanalysis and education was realized in the work of Aichhorn and his colleagues at a unique school for delinquent young people in Vienna. Extending the concepts of psychoanalytic education from children able to manage in society to those troubled young people requiring group care, Aichhorn described an effort to create an environment in which socially disruptive actions could be understood rather than judged, and in which young people could be helped to understand the reasons and causes for their anti-social activity. Following clinical psychoanalytic perspectives, Aichhorn stressed the importance of staff becoming aware of their own responses to young people as essential in work with troubled young people.

This perspective was well exemplified in the work of Anna Freud, first in the Freud-Rosenfeld School in Vienna, and later at the Hampstead Clinic in London (now the Anna Freud Center). Providing intensive education in the psychoanalytic psychology of teaching and learning, child development, and the therapeutic process, Miss Freud and her colleagues explored the significance of the psychoanalytic perspective in both the classroom and the consulting room. Miss Freud's school in Vienna, founded on the principles of her father, together with the educational philosophy of John Dewey and Maria

[Haworth co-indexing entry note]: "Foreword." Cohler, Bertram J. Co-published simultaneously in *Residential Treatment for Children & Youth* (The Haworth Press, Inc.) Vol. 18, No. 2, 2000, pp. xvii-xx; and: *The Forsaken Child: Essays on Group Care and Individual Therapy* (D. Patrick Zimmerman) The Haworth Press, Inc., 2000, pp. xi-xiv. Single or multiple copies of this article are available for a fee from The Haworth Document Delivery Service [1-800-342-9678, 9:00 a.m. - 5:00 p.m. (EST). E-mail address: getinfo@haworthpressinc.com].

Montessori, included such collaborators as Peter Blos and Erik Erikson. This tradition was carried on in the post-war period in the United States by a group of educators whose own formative professional experience had been with Miss Freud and Aichhorn in their pioneering educational experiences in Vienna. First in Detroit, and later at the National Institute of Mental Health, Fritz Redl created a residential school founded on the model of Aichhorn's earlier efforts in Vienna. Together with David Wineman, Redl wrote two critical volumes, *Children Who Hate* (1951) and *Controls from Within* (1952), which expanded upon the approach advocated by Aichhorn for working with delinquent young people.

Perhaps the most detailed and complete integration of the Viennese perspective on psychoanalysis and education was provided by Bruno Bettelheim, who undertook direction of a residential school, then a part of The University of Chicago. Bettelheim's work echoed many of the same themes as those of Aichhorn and Redl and Wineman. However, to a much greater extent than either the Viennese work or that of Redl and Wineman, Bettelheim realized the significance of all aspects of the world in which the children lived as elements of the therapeutic process. Writing about milieu therapy in a much more detailed and inclusive manner than sometimes used since his formative work, Bettelheim showed that children make meanings of even such apparently insignificant aspects of their environment as the decor of hallways and stairways. He also showed the importance to the curative process of *all* staff working at the Orthogenic School.

From the cooks and the housekeepers, to the seamstress, to the staff providing direct child care, every interaction with a child or with each other was seen as significant in helping to undo the impact of life-circumstances experienced by the children as overwhelming and beyond their control. Bettelheim's effort was to create a world in which the children felt safe and well-cared for, and in which they would not feel overwhelmed and out of control within a system of roles, rules, and organizational structure forcing compliance and manipulation. Recognizing the power of the environment to change personality for ill, as in the Nazi concentration camps in which he had been an inmate in the middle 1930s, as well as the dangers of a mass society to enforce compliance at the cost of sense of personal initiative, Bettelheim sought to create an environment fostering a sense of autonomy and personal responsibility.

The perspective of Redl and Wineman, and of Bettelheim, was successful in providing for the education of troubled children. The tragedy of the past three decades in which concern with management of psychological treatment by managed care has taken precedence over the best interests of children is that there are now all too few places where troubled children can receive the sophisticated and understanding care provided by these pioneers of psychoanalytic education. However, recent reports from the Research Department of the Orthogenic School point to the continuing need for such a perspective. Extending the tradition of the earlier pioneers in milieu therapy, Patrick Zimmerman has demonstrated the continued salience of this perspective in work with troubled youth in contemporary society. Reporting on work with those young people so well portrayed by Redl and Wineman as the children no one wants, often termed children with "primary attachment disorders," Zimmerman shows that it is possible to help these young people to resume forward development and to overcome a traumatic past through provision of individual treatment and group care founded on the concepts of psychoanalytic education.

Zimmerman is a particularly incisive observer of children, which is truly in the tradition of Bettelheim's own unique capacity to understand the lives of troubled young people. With originality, zest for clinical scholarship and acuity of observation of the lives of these very troubled children in residential care, perhaps without parallel since Bettelheim's own pioneering work, Zimmerman makes a cogent and compelling argument for the continuation of the concept of psychoanalytic therapeutic milieu. Zimmerman is a very gifted clinician and writer. Beyond these skills, Zimmerman explicates a paradigm for work with seriously troubled youngsters which could be emulated in other settings. His essay on psychotherapy in residential treatment is a movingly persuasive call for psychoanalysis to once more accept its mission of compassionate clinical understanding as a prelude to psychotherapeutic intervention. That essay points to the public policy implications of the present failure to provide adequate care for seriously troubled young people, whose lives could be forever changed through the devoted work of those committed to the tradition, concepts and methods of the psychoanalytic residential milieu. Zimmerman is able to demonstrate the power of this perspective in two wonderfully written and compelling case studies. Zimmerman shows through richly detailed discussion the significance of a psychoanalytic individual treatment and milieu perspective for enabling even the most troubled children to resume psychological development and to realize marked success as a result of the care provided within a milieu dedicated to work with these troubled young people.

Bertram J. Cohler, PhD
The University of Chicago

REFERENCES

Aichhorn, A. (1925). *Wayward Youth.* (Trans. E. Bryant, J. Deming, M. O'Neil, G. Hawkins, G. Mohr, E. Mohr, H. Ross and H. Thun). New York: The Viking Press.

Freud, S. (1925/1961). Preface to Aichhorn's *Wayward Youth.* In. J. Strachey (Ed.) *The Standard Edition of the Complete Psychological Works of Sigmund Freud, 19,* London: Hogarth Press and the Institute for Psychoanalysis, pps. 273-275.

Redl, F., Wineman, D. (1951). *Children Who Hate.* New York: The Free Press/Macmillan.

Redl, F., Wineman, D. (1952). *Controls from Within.* New York: The Free Press/Macmillan.

Preface

For many years, a number of mental health professionals, public interest groups, and child advocates have been pressing for the use of increasingly time-limited models of residential treatment and psychotherapy for children and adolescents. Despite the reservations of many who influence the direction of child welfare national public policy about longer term, more intensive models of care for young people, we are faced with the paradox that at the same time the children who are most often presently referred for residential care are clearly more emotionally disturbed, have more extensive backgrounds of social failure and have dysfunctional or barely existent families.

Confronted with this dilemma, the following selected essays on the delivery of group care and individual treatment services for young people present an argument for the preservation of more thoughtful, humanistic forms of residential treatment and psychotherapy for children and adolescents. The introductory article, *Youth in Residential Care: From War Nursery to Therapeutic Milieu*, presents an examination of Anna Freud's five-year altruistic devotion to providing group care for the infant and child victims of the World War II bombings of London. At the same time, the article describes important parallels between Miss Freud's observations of the young war victims in her care and the experiences of hundreds of thousands of abandoned, neglected, or abused children in our American cities today. The following article, *From Disciplinary Control to Benign Milieu in Children's Residential Treatment*, traces the historical foundations of milieu treatment from August Aichhorn and Anna Freud in Europe, to the early pioneering efforts of Fritz Redl and Bruno Bettelheim in the United States. It presents a detailed examination of Bettelheim's posi-

[Haworth co-indexing entry note]: "Preface." Co-published simultaneously in *Residential Treatment for Children & Youth* (The Haworth Press, Inc.) Vol. 18, No. 2, 2000, pp. xxi-xxii; and: *The Forsaken Child: Essays on Group Care and Individual Therapy* (D. Patrick Zimmerman) The Haworth Press, Inc., 2000, pp. xv-xvi. Single or multiple copies of this article are available for a fee from The Haworth Document Delivery Service [1-800-342-9678, 9:00 a.m. - 5:00 p.m. (EST). E-mail address: getinfo@haworthpressinc.com].

xv

tive theoretical contributions to our understanding of milieu therapy, as well as a discussion of persisting issues in our attempts to understand the details of group care and the difficulties involved in providing individual therapy to young people within a group care setting.

Psychotherapy in Residential Treatment: The Human Toll of Scientism and Managed Care compares the humane concerns of the early founders of residential care with the present-day climate, which emphasizes the objectivist models for proof of treatment efficacy. The demands for empirical evaluation are discussed in terms of the scientistic attacks upon the conceptual foundations of dynamic psychotherapy, and in light of the historical emergence of managed care as a controlling power over the delivery of mental health services. The discussion in this article concludes with a reconsideration of those objectivist attacks in light of contemporary refinements in psychoanalytic theory, conceptions of the human mind, and ideas about modern culture.

The selection of essays concludes with a presentation of two extended clinical case presentations. *The Little Turtle's Progress: On Psychotherapy in Residential Treatment* provides a detailed description of a long-term individual psychotherapy case of a young child in residential care, indicating a number of clinical issues which appear to contraindicate the use of either brief therapy techniques or short-term group care. Finally, *Desperation and Hope in the Analysis of a "Thrown-Away" Adolescent Boy* presents an extended commentary on the successful psychoanalysis of an abandoned, depressed, often rageful adolescent boy in residential care. Given the boy's ongoing experiences of desperation and hopelessness, the article describes how an interactive, social-constructivist treatment approach helped to foster the boy's psychological growth and sense of optimism about the future.

D. Patrick Zimmerman, PsyD
The Sonia Shankman Orthogenic School
The University of Chicago

Youth in Residential Care:
From War Nursery to Therapeutic Milieu

Bertram J. Cohler, PhD
D. Patrick Zimmerman, PsyD

SUMMARY. The issue of violence in childhood and society is re-viewed from the comparative perspective of the care of children by Anna Freud and her colleagues during the bombing of World War II and the plight of seriously troubled children and adolescents living in pov-erty and in violent families in contemporary society. Violence among these children is understood as a response to a world experience that is depleting and overwhelming; some sense of being alive is provided through aggressive behavior. It is proposed that the concepts of the therapeutic milieu as originally elaborated by Aichhorn, Bettelheim, and Redl and Wineman remain valuable in our present-day efforts to foster enhanced capacity for tension management and ego development via techniques of crisis management within the group living situation, incorporating the life-space or marginal interview, therapeutic educa-tion, and psychotherapy. *[Article copies available for a fee from The Haworth Document Delivery Service: 1-800-342-9678. E-mail address: <getinfo@haworth pressinc.com> Website: <http://www.HaworthPress.com>]*

KEYWORDS. Anna Freud, residential treatment, psychoanalysis

An extended version of this paper was previously published in *The Psychoanalyt-ic Study of the Child, 52*, Albert J. Solnit, Peter B. Neubauer, Samuel Abrams, and A. Scott Dowling (Eds.). Yale University Press, copyright 1997. Permission for reprint was granted by Yale University Press.

[Haworth co-indexing entry note]: "Youth in Residential Care: From War Nursery to Therapeutic Milieu." Cohler, Bertram J., and D. Patrick Zimmerman. Co-published simultaneously in *Residential Treatment for Children & Youth* (The Haworth Press, Inc.) Vol. 18, No. 2, 2000, pp. 1-25; and: *The Forsaken Child: Essays on Group Care and Individual Therapy* (D. Patrick Zimmerman) The Haworth Press, Inc., 2000, pp. 1-25. Single or multiple copies of this article are available for a fee from The Haworth Document Delivery Service [1-800-342-9678, 9:00 a.m. - 5:00 p.m. (EST). E-mail address: getinfo@haworthpressinc. com].

INTRODUCTION

Western Europe and the United States are unique among the world's cultures in their focus on the immediate family as not only the primary source of socialization but also the most important source of care. Both developmental studies and public policy emphasize a household consisting of two parents and their children. But too often the reality is that disrupted family life is more characteristic of the experiences of young children, particularly those living in poverty, than is a stable immediate family (Demos, 1986; Coontz, 1992).

The widespread belief that children's development is inevitably enhanced by residence in a so-called family environment is also challenged by harsh reality. We propose an alternative view: for children experiencing significant psychological scars as a consequence of continuing neglect and physical and sexual abuse, we believe that residential care in a milieu designed to facilitate the expectable course of development can provide a better solution, including a sense of mastery and personal integrity and enhanced capacity for close and satisfying personal relationships.

One of the earliest models for this kind of residential care was developed by Anna Freud and her colleagues during World War II. Anna Freud and Dorothy Burlingham provided a safe residential setting where young children endangered by the bombing of central London could receive high-quality care in a group setting outside the immediate zone of destruction. Their reports on the children under their care and their discussion of problems of separation from and reunion with parents, children's experiences with group life, and staff responses to the children are highly relevant to children in American cities today.

Children in urban areas regularly confront violence and personal abuse perhaps even more destructive to personality development than the senseless bombing of the war was to their counterparts fifty years ago. For example, one child was watching television in his apartment in a high-rise inner-city housing development when two bullets shattered his bedroom window and nearly hit him. His mother plugged the bullet holes with incense, which had the additional effect of covering the smells of urine and excrement emanating from the outside corridor. Nationwide, incidents of child abuse and neglect have reached nearly epidemic proportions (National Research Council, 1993); Cicchetti and Barnett (1991) report a rate of 22.6 per 1,000 children, a two-thirds increase in less than a decade. From 1980 to 1990, reported cases of physical abuse increased by 58 percent, and reported cases of sexual abuse increased 300 percent. Clearly, these dramatic increases are greater than can be accounted for by better reporting mechanisms. Among all the cases of physical and sexual abuse reported to authorities, more than half involve physical neglect or abandonment of infants and young children (Sedlak, 1988, 1991).

This alarming national increase in cases of reported child maltreatment is reflected in the caseloads of child-care services in the United States, which currently have responsibility for hundreds of thousands of abandoned, neglected, or abused children. Removal of these children from their homes to group living situations offering safety and comfort is as important to their development as was the protection of an earlier generation of endangered children from the air attacks on London. In situations where domestic violence is a fact of everyday life, where gang warfare and the sounds of gunfire provide a frightening background for their attempts to sleep, today's children, like the London children who tried to sleep despite the sounds of attack, experience a sense of dread.

THE WAR NURSERY AS A THERAPEUTIC MILIEU

In 1940, when Nazis initiated their bombing of London, Anna Freud became concerned for the physical safety and psychological security of young children exposed to this violence. Her first efforts to develop a temporary shelter for these children were soon replaced by a more ambitious scheme involving residence programs in Hampstead and in the countryside. Anna Freud's close friend and collaborator Dorothy Burlingham was then in New York, where she persuaded the American Foster Parents' Plan to agree to fund the war nursery project (Young-Bruehl, 1988). Over the next five years, the war nursery project became not only an important shelter for London's children but also an important center for the training of a generation of child analysts and an important laboratory for the study of infant and child development. Volume 3 of *The Writings of Anna Freud* (Freud & Burlingham, [1944] 1973) contains not only the classic work *Infants Without Families: The Case for and Against Residential Nurseries* (Freud & Burlingham, [1944] 1973) but also a complete compilation of the monthly reports to the Foster Parents' Plan from February 1941 through December 1945. These reports offer detailed observations on child development, children's responses to separation and loss, the development of group life in a residential school, the problems of maintaining contact with parents, psychological contagion within the residential group, and the relationship of children and their workers. Many of these issues apply not only to the work of the war nurseries but also more generally to the residential education of children and adolescents today.

The monthly reports to the American foundation and the more extended discussion in the 1944 monograph document Miss Freud's struggle to maintain contact with the families of the children in her care. The residences were kept open at all hours so that parents could come to see their children whenever possible. While many parents made every effort to visit, others found that work schedules, other family responsibilities, and the inevitable wartime family separations posed insuperable obstacles. And a few parents, Miss Freud observed, enjoyed their newfound freedom from the responsibility for day-to-day child care and found it difficult to accept their children back into the home at the war's end.

The consequences of the separation of family and child for the child's development posed an issue for residential care then as now.[1] Freud and Burlingham ([1944] 1973), acknowledging the contributions of August Aichhorn,[2] noted the danger that children who spend long periods of time in care outside of the family may all too readily become "institutionalized"–that is, adjusted to the demands of the milieu– and may fail to develop a sense of individuality and purpose. Accordingly, Aichhorn explicitly cautioned against forcing children to adjust to rules designed to serve the needs of the institution rather than the children.[3]

Freud and Burlingham observed the children's tendency to regress when they entered residential care after having lived most of their life at home. They noted that consistent care provided by a few workers with whom the children had developed a relationship was critical in preventing children from becoming institutionalized. Indeed, the relationship between child and care giver was the best predictor of success in residential care. At the same time, the staff of a psychoanalytically oriented residential center, they believed, may be able to resolve particular impasses in the child's development that are a consequence of unresolved issues in the parents' psychological development.

Freud and her colleagues documented the problems within the group itself as children learn to live together. When children live together, the group takes on a life of its own; as early as 1921, Sigmund Freud had observed the power of groups over the individual: "An individual in a group is subjected through its influence to what is often a profound alteration in his mental activity. His liability to affect becomes extraordinarily intensified, while his intellectual ability is markedly reduced" (p. 88). In an observational study the psychologist Kurt Lewin (1951) suggested that "emotional contagion" was a major issue in group life. When groups of even young children live together, a supraindividual personality develops, which in large measure governs the actions of group members (Redl & Wineman, 1951, 1952). Children with charismatic qualities are particularly able to influence the group. Consistent with Freud's ([1921] 1955) observations regarding the roles of leader and group, group work in a residential setting requires that these dynamics be clarified in an effort to help children understand their motivation to follow the leader. Identification and the feeling of enhanced personal integrity realized from joining one's energies with those of the leader (Kohut, 1985) are as important for children's groups as for groups of adults.

ANNA FREUD'S WRITINGS ON THE WAR NURSERIES

It is beyond the scope of this essay to examine in detail the broad range of issues discussed in the initial reports on the Hampstead war nurseries. Instead, we will briefly note the special historical importance of Anna Freud's war nursery writings and then give a summary of their purpose, organization, and clinical discussions.

Historical Significance

First, the war nursery studies testify to Anna Freud's five-year devotion to the residential care of infant and child victims of World War II. From this perspective, they are a monument to what Young-Bruehl (1988) has described as a major source of Anna Freud's seemingly tireless emotional strength–her enduring sense of altruism. Anna Freud's immersion in the daily work of caring for the real and "artificial" infant and child orphans of war also suggests a number of other personal and professional motivations. For example, her initial commitment to creating the nurseries and her near-total devotion during the war to the residential care of children suffering from wartime parental separation or loss can be understood at one level as an important way of coping with her own feelings of grief over the recent death of her father. The war nursery effort also represented Anna Freud's reunion with her life companion and professional colleague, Dorothy Burlingham. During their five years of caring for infants and young children separated from their families, Freud and Burlingham had the opportunity to create detailed developmental records on the children. This afforded Anna Freud the invaluable opportunity to translate Freud's psychosexual theories of child development, based on psychoanalytic reconstruction and hypothesis, into writings based on actual child observations and thus to demonstrate and affirm her father's view of infantile and child development in terms of the super ordinate position of drive and libido. At the same time, the war nursery, along with Anna Freud's private Wednesday seminars and the training program for workers at the Hampstead war nursery, served as a forum from which to respond to the theoretical differences raised by the followers of Melanie Klein in the British Psychoanalytic Society.

Finally, their experiences in and writings about the war nurseries made rich contributions to the broader areas of psychoanalytic training and research. For example, the early war nursery training program led to the development of an alternative Freudian track for candidates in training at the British Psychoanalytic Society and eventually evolved into a full-scale, certified psychoanalytic training course. In addition, responding to Ernst Kris's advice that she make her writing a priority rather than continue to expend her energies on frustrating political struggles with the Kleinian faction, Anna Freud in 1944 enthusiastically lent her support to the establishment of a yearly psychoanalytic journal being organized by Kris in New York. She hoped that this annual, *The Psychoanalytic Study of the Child*, would serve as a medium for presenting the child research she had begun in the war nurseries.

Clinical Contributions

Each of the monthly reports on the war nurseries usually presented statistics on enrollment, health, food, and clinical problems observed during the month. As already noted, the war nursery work and the writings on it are indebted to Anna Freud's great friend August Aichhorn and his study of the residential treatment of delinquent adolescents, *Wayward Youth* (Aichhorn, 1925). Aichhorn's book was largely devoted to describing the creation of a benevolent residential milieu and specific treatment interventions and techniques. However, the case histories he supplied make it clear that many of the youth had suffered early maternal loss or deprivation. Thus a close reading of *Wayward Youth* reveals the overriding importance of the mother-child relationship and Aichhorn's conviction that disturbances in that relationship lead to antisocial symptoms or behaviors: "The great majority of children in need of retraining come into conflict with society because of an unsatisfied need for tenderness and love in their childhood. We therefore find in them a proportionately increased thirst for pleasure and for primitive forms of instinctual gratification. They lack inhibitions and they have a strong, though distorted, craving for affection. If the delinquency is to be cured rather than repressed, we must meet these needs even though at first this seems futile to so-called understanding people" (pp. 148-49). Aichhorn also observed that "most of these young people have never had their infantile needs for affection satisfied. They have never experienced the happiness of a close relationship to the mother. They need love" (p. 152).

In her war nursery writings, Anna Freud focused more specifically on children's reactions to separation from parental figures, especially the mother, in terms of differing developmental stages. She noted that observers seldom appreciate the depth and seriousness of the feelings of grief aroused by maternal separation during the second year of the child's life: "Reactions to parting at this time of life are particularly violent. The child feels suddenly deserted by all the known persons in his world to whom he has learned to attach importance. His new ability to love finds itself deprived of the accustomed objects, and his greed for affection remains unsatisfied. His longing for his mother becomes intolerable and throws him into states of despair which are very similar to the despair and distress shown by babies who are hungry and whose food does not appear at the accustomed time. For several hours or even for a day or two this psychological craving of the child, the 'hunger' for his mother, may override all bodily sensations" ([1941-45] 1973, pp. 182-83).

Children older than three seem to have a more complex reaction to maternal separation, experiencing it as the dangerous result of negative feelings they may have had or expressed about the parent:

Children [in this phase] are quick in their anger and know only one main punishment for anybody who offends them, i.e., that this person should go away and not return, which in childish language means that he should die. . . . It does not seem so very dangerous to kill a parent in fantasy if at the same time outward evidence shows that this same parent is alive and well . . . but separation seems to be an intolerable confirmation of all these negative feelings. Father and mother are now really gone. The child is frightened by their absence and suspects that their desertion may be another punishment or even the consequence of his own bad wishes. To overcome this guilt he over stresses all the love which he has ever felt for his parents. This turns the natural pain of separation into an intense longing which is hard to bear. . . . The negative feelings . . . undergo repression and create all sorts of moods and problems of behavior, the origin of which remains unknown to child and worker alike. (pp. 188-89, 191)

Elsewhere in this book, Anna Freud hypothesized about the longer term psychosocial effects of maternal loss on the child. She lamented that in a time of family dissolution and environmental violence, child care services, originally viewed as supportive extensions of the family, were transformed into a substitute for the family. Thus the residential programs created by the wartime emergencies were suddenly called on to provide "all the functions of child welfare rolled into one . . . in wartime the nursery, even if not residential, becomes a foster home" (p. 126). As such, the "nursery" and residential center had to provide much more than programs of ordinary education; they had to expand their missions to include the functions of both a convalescent home and a school for problem children. And the most difficult of those functions, Anna Freud said, was "to lessen the shock of the breaking up of family life and to find–during the absence from the mother–a really good substitute for the mother relationship" (p. 127).

According to Anna Freud, without ongoing, caring emotional relations with the parents, the child becomes vulnerable to long-term developmental difficulties and may suffer an impairment in the ability to develop deep and mutual love relationships later in life. Further, the capacity to endure the demands of education depends crucially on conditions of parental love, for the child can endure the restrictions inherent in the educational process only if he or she has the underlying conviction that the limitations placed on the gratification of primitive needs in the name of education will result in parental approval and love.

At the end of the first year's work in the war nurseries, Anna Freud (Report # 12, pp. 156-212) summarized her observations of the children's reactions, both cognitive and emotional, to witnessing actual war destruction, including the dissolution of the family. She began with a discussion of how difficult it was for young children to understand why they were being evacuated and separated from their mothers. This cognitive difficulty is compounded, of course, when the young child must make sense of the death of a family member from whom he or she had already been separated.

She then turned to a consideration of the young child's reactions to an environment characterized by violence and destruction. Surprisingly, in children who had witnessed and experienced the ravages of war, the psychological danger lay not in traumatic shock but elsewhere:

> The real danger is not that the child, caught up all innocently in the whirlpool of the war, will be shocked into illness. The danger lies in the fact that the destruction raging in the outer world may meet the very real aggressiveness which rages in the inside of the child. At the age when education should start to deal with these impulses, confirmation should not be given from the outside world that the same impulses are uppermost in other people. . . . It must be very difficult for them [children] to accomplish this task of fighting their own death wishes when, at the same time, people are killed and hurt every day around them. Children have to be safeguarded against the primitive horrors of the war, not because horrors and atrocities are so strange to them, but because we want them at this decisive stage of their development to overcome and estrange themselves from the primitive and atrocious wishes of their own infantile nature. (pp. 162-63)

Freud then described the various types of anxiety she had observed in the nursery children. She noted that the children's fears of air raids were neither universal nor as overwhelming as might have been expected. To explain why the anxiety was present in some cases and absent in others, mild for most children but violent in certain children, she proposed a schema of five types of anxiety—all, of course, far different from Klein's basic conception of infantile anxiety: (1) anxiety as a response to some real danger present in the external world; (2) anxiety provoked by the potential outburst of certain forbidden instinctual wishes; (3) anxiety related to the fear of authority and punishment; (4) anxiety based on sharing the fear reactions of their mothers and the grown-up world around them; and (5) anxiety reactions to current situations (such as an air raid), which become associated with a past loss (for example, the wartime death of a father).

Anna Freud concluded her review by examining the ego functioning of her charges in terms of some of the most commonly utilized coping and defense mechanisms, or "normal and abnormal methods of outlet." She noted that many of the psychological methods and outlets available to adults for dealing with danger are not yet available to the young child. Some outlets for fears and anxiety are available, however, including speech, play activities, behavioral enactments, fantasy life, regression, and the return to more infantile modes of functioning (such as bed wetting, autoerotic forms of gratification, greed and aggression, temper tantrums, and the abnormal withdrawal of emotional interest from the external world).

RESIDENTIAL TREATMENT AND CHILDREN OF TRAUMA

The second part of the war nursery writings, *Infants Without Families: The Case for and Against Residential Nurseries* (Freud & Burlingham, [1944] 1973), can be read as a conceptual overview of the fifty-six monthly reports, focusing largely on the clinical problems raised in those reports and presenting the authors' conclusions regarding the advantages and disadvantages of residential care as compared with normal family relations. The residential setting appeared to have an advantage over the average low-income family in the basic health care and feeding of infants under five months of age, but the advantage shifts to the family for children from five to twelve months of age, especially in the capacity for emotional interplay. From one to two years of age, residential children benefit more in the areas of gross motor development and eating habits, but they lag behind family children in speech development and toilet training. Freud and Burlingham felt that in general the residential child has advantages over the family child in areas of development that are independent of the emotional part of life. However, they concluded that the residential child appeared to be at a clear disadvantage whenever the child's emotional relationship with the mother and the family was a crucial or determinant factor for a particular developmental achievement.

The issues of attachment to and separation from parents and the principles for the construction of children's groups which emerged from the work of Freud and Burlingham during World War II remain relevant for the care of children in contemporary urban society at risk because of new forms of violence within both family and community. Earlier studies sought to apply the concepts and methods of the psychoanalytic approach to treatment, research, and intervention with children at risk for personal distress as a consequence of social disorganization. From Aichhorn's (1925) pioneering study of delinquent youth, to Redl and Wineman's (1951, 1952) explorations of the impact of social disorganization on ego development, to Pavenstedt's (1967) study of socially disorganized families, the significance of psychoanalysis both as a perspective on developmental processes and as a method of study has been shown to be paramount. Freud ([1913] 1955) observed that among all the applications of psychoanalysis, education was the most important. His observation regarding the significance of psychoanalysis for understanding mental life, derived from intensive study of life in schools, sparked increased interest in this application in the period following World War I.

In *Wayward Youth*, the first intensive study of antisocial behavior among youth, Aichhorn argued that the roots of antisocial actions could be understood from a psychoanalytic perspective, not just at the level of metapsychology, as Freud ([1915] 1955, [1920] 1955) had shown, but also at the level of behavior. The collection of articles on Aichhorn's work edited by Eissler (1949) includes several contributions describing the use of the psychoanalytic perspective in the treatment of violent offenders.

Building on Aichhorn's effort to understand aggression from a psychodynamic perspective, Redl and Wineman (1951) provided a cogent perspective on the development of impulse control for the "ego that cannot perform," in order to enhance the capacity for tolerating frustration and coping with insecurity, anxiety, and fear, to increase resistance to temptation, and to foster sublimation. Later studies attempted to extend the psychodynamic understanding of violence from the individual child to the larger community. The study of the North Point Project in Boston by Pavenstedt and her colleagues (1967) demonstrated the salience of understanding lives from the perspective of both personal experience and community characteristics, and documents the impact of living in poverty on the experiences of self and others. Preoccupied parents placed their own needs before the best interests of the child and responded to even minimal frustration with rage, which interfered with family life and perpetuated patterns of violence into the next generation. Some parents had inadequate models for raising children. Extreme poverty also affected cognitive functions; Pavenstedt and her colleagues reported significant problems in communication among the parents and delays in language learning among the children. Some parents found it difficult to instruct their children about how to manage even the most mundane aspects of daily life; difficulties in impulse control made it hard to solve problems in a systematic manner. Most significantly, Pavenstedt and her colleagues observed that:

> . . . the mothers often engaged in unpredictable, aggressive, violent outbursts and impulsive acting out. This behavior itself was traumatic for the children but became increasingly traumatic because of the mothers' undifferentiated relationship to their children. An act of violence against one child could occur just because that child was nearby when the real target of the aggression and the offender was another child. Because they [the mothers] lacked the education and models for control of impulses, they had developed little control and brought neglect, cruelty, and primitive sexual behavior into the family life. These dangers, coupled with the aggressive sexual activity of the neighbors and the brutality of the environment, were central in the failure of the children to develop impulse control. The institutions in the community finally compounded the danger with their punitive attitudes toward poor people as retaliation for consequences of uncontrolled drive behavior. (p. 236)

Stack (1974) reported similar observations in her study of multigenerational families living in abject poverty.

In contemporary American society, with oftentimes limited employment opportunities for many families, a welfare system in tatters, and an epidemic of unplanned pregnancies among underclass adolescent girls, many families suffer terrible privation. Children born into these circumstances, particularly girls, are vulnerable to abuse, especially in the first decade of life (Aday, 1993). Indeed, economic hardship may emerge as the single most powerful predictor of the need for protective services for children. The callousness of contemporary society toward those less fortunate can spark rage. Children of this class grow up lacking the experience of self-coherence, personal integrity, or identity and may seek violence as a desperate means of affirming that they are still alive (Terman, 1975). The despair evoked by such extreme misfortune magnifies the hostility evident among many parents of young children, who all too often respond with acts of sexual and physical abuse. From earliest infancy their children suffer neglect by adults preoccupied with issues of getting by each day and resolving the many personal and familial conflicts they face (Aday, 1993). All too often, parental feelings of being overwhelmed and terrified lead to the enactment of brutality against the infant, whose demands for care are experienced as intolerable. Zigler and Hall (1989) reported that nearly all American parents use corporal punishment in the home. A study by Straus et al. (1980) found that more than half of adolescents had been punished with physical violence in the preceding year. Further, teachers share the parents' belief that physical punishment may be required in order to subdue and train children. We are unlikely to reduce violence in society as long as angry adults continue to take out their frustrations on their children and induct yet another generation into the violence characteristic of our society.

American society remains the most violent in the community of industrialized nations. Even when we recognize differences in reporting crimes, the rate of crime in the United States is among the highest in the world and is particularly notable for sexual and other forms of assault (Reiss & Roth, 1993).[4] The United States is the only industrialized nation that still enforces the death penalty and the only one in which homicides annually exceed all deaths from illness among persons under age thirty. From the Revolutionary War to the Civil War (perhaps the most costly war in terms of human lives recorded to date), American life has been founded on the assumption that there are evil forces impinging on the community which must be responded to in kind.

The contradiction is that Americans maintain a belief in the importance of compassion toward those who are vulnerable–the very young and the very old–while the rates of violence perpetrated by family members against the young and the old continue to rise (Straus et al., 1980). Our society is characterized by both anxiety regarding parenthood and hostility toward dependent offspring (Whiting, 1963; Minturn & Lambert, 1964; Gil, 1970; Belsky, 1980). As Garbarino (1979), Hobbs (1980), and Kaufman and Zigler (1989) all have noted, it should hardly be surprising that such a violent society inflicts particular violence on those who are most vulnerable,[5] or that adults most suffering environmental and personal deprivation all too often take out their depression and rage on children (Pavenstedt, 1967; Downey & Coyne, 1990; Belsky, 1993). A cycle of physical abuse and neglect is all too common in many underclass families. The hope that aunts, cousins, or grandparents might assist with child care proves futile, since these relatives also are stressed (Banfield, 1958; Stack, 1974). Ultimately, the children become wards of the state, often after formal complaints have been filed against the parents for neglect or as a consequence of wanton abandonment.

An early history of maltreatment can significantly impair the development of these children (Redl & Wineman, 1951, 1952). As a consequence, placement in foster care generally proves unworkable. With diminished ability to maintain attachment and the experience of intrusive affects which disrupt both thought and action, such infants grow into a vulnerable childhood, showing so-called conduct or behavioral disorders from an early age. These children are so profoundly troubled that they disrupt the classroom as well as the home. Many of them end up in children's shelters because there is no other place for them in the community.

Life in these grim shelters is little better than life on the streets. Overcrowding obliges many children to make their beds under the desks of welfare officers. The refusal of state legislatures to fund children's care properly has created a situation of crisis at the same time that there is increasing demand for the care of these children.[6] Suits brought against state agencies responsible for the care of children have led to very modest increases in funding for children's services. An environment as carefully structured as the war nurseries may provide the only hope for these children's resumption of the expectable course of development and resolution of their distress.

WORKING WITH THE CHILDREN OF DESPAIR

Recent studies, particularly those in the tradition of self-psychology pioneered by D. W. Winnicott (1953, 1960a), George Klein (1976), and Heinz Kohut and his associates (Kohut, 1971, 1972, 1977, 1984; Terman, 1975; Elson, 1986; Wolf, 1988; Marohn, 1993), have questioned the applicability of a drive perspective in understanding aggression and have posed an alternative formulation based on concern with personal integrity. Indeed, Marohn (1993) suggested that much destructive behavior in family and society can be understood as the product of a "contentless" rage evoked by the feeling of not having been responded to by others and by the larger society. It is imperative that we better understand the impact of this early trauma on the lives of children and that we develop sufficiently sturdy intervention programs to turn around developmental processes currently leading to lives of distress and despair.

Clinical and quantitative studies have shown that children who experience early physical neglect and abuse are likely to become aggressive and to react unpredictably to even minor changes in the daily routine. Physical abuse is particularly likely to lead to behavior characterized as "acting out," constant anger, and aggression (Dodge et al., 1990; National Research Council, 1993). This behavior is less a reflection of adult aggressive behavior than a personal response to the feeling of being overwhelmed in a world that has become unmanageable (Bettelheim, 1943; Marohn, 1993). Clinically, the children appear to be conduct-disordered and have problems complying with rules and routines. They are likely to be disadvantaged in their capacity for relating to other children or maintaining a sense of competence. Children exposed to sexual abuse show, in addition, problems in maintaining attention and may experience dissociative states that interfere in the development of a sense of personal integrity or coherence (Straus & Gelles, 1990; Trickett & Putnam, 1994). Such children often are able to resist or overcome the effects of medication that otherwise has been shown to be effective among children with psychiatric disorders. In our own time, the term "post-traumatic stress disorder," originally applied to personnel returning home from the Vietnam conflict, has been applied to these children of despair.

FROM COMMUNITY TO RESIDENTIAL CARE

While children in the war nurseries came from circumstances of externally imposed violence, children referred for residential treatment today come from situations of violence within the family. Large numbers of them have been physically abused by a parent and often sexually abused as well; physical neglect is common. The children experience this abusive "care" as a traumatic shock in which external danger articulates with dangers stemming from the child's own impulses. Indeed, sexual abuse may be without parallel in stimulating anxiety regarding forbidden wishes.

Most of the children enrolled in the war nurseries came from a family and showed a strong negative response to separation and developmental organization at marked variance from their actual ages. Children in residential care today come from families, foster or group homes, or psychiatric hospitals or shelters. Many grow to young adulthood in this group setting and leave the school for higher education or work having spent little of their childhood within a family. There appear to be two modes of response to relocation and separation. Observations of children who come to residential care from a family environment are consistent with the observations of children in the war nurseries group regarding the desire to remain at home regardless of the physical or psychological dangers that living at home might present. For example, despite coming from a home in which a parent was physically abusive, a child might well spend the first weeks away from home full of rage at the separation, to the surprise of the staff members. But to a child removed from the only home he or she has ever known and from the constancy of the mother, separation is a particular problem. Retreat to earlier developmental stages is common among such children. They react to separation with expressions of rage rather than with physical symptoms or renewed emphasis on earlier developmental gains.

Among children who have spent much time in group homes, separation and enrollment at a residential care facility can have a much less dramatic impact. These children express feelings of resignation and despair. The residential center appears to be one more in a long string of placements. Anna Freud's writings on the war nurseries, following Aichhorn's initial concern, stressed the importance of avoiding a sense of "institutionalization," with its impact on conformity to rules and externalization of all problems. Children coming to residential care from repeated and lengthy placements show the impact of institutionalization and may often resist efforts to foster an increased sense of competence.

Anna Freud noted that among young children talking about danger and enacting it are characteristic methods of dealing with violence. For older children, aggression and temper tantrums are among the most significant modes of coping with traumatic shock created by violence. As Miss Freud (1972) observed:

> It is a common misunderstanding of the child's nature which leads people to suppose that children will be saddened by the sight of destruction and aggression . . . the more their strength and independence are growing, the more they will have to be watched so as not to create too much damage, not to hurt each other or those weaker than themselves. We often say, half-jokingly, that there is a continual war raging in a nursery . . . the destruction raging in the outer world may be the real aggressiveness which rages inside the child . . . they fight against their own wishes to do away with people of whom they are jealous, who disturb or disappoint them, or who offend their childish feelings some other way. It must be very difficult for them to accomplish this task of fighting their own death wishes when, at the same time, people are being hurt and killed around them. (p. 163)

This observation regarding the child's response to violence is consistent with much contemporary literature (Patterson, 1982; Dodge et al., 1990, Gelles, 1992) on the intergenerational transmission of violence and abuse within impoverished families. It is common for children in group care who were born into circumstances of abuse and neglect to respond with rage to circumstances that most children would be able to master with little difficulty. An unusually complex problem in arithmetic or some unexpected change in plans is likely to precipitate acts of destructive aggression. The violence these children suffered for so long has honed their own death wishes to a fine edge; it is difficult for them to contain their own aggression. Efforts in residential care to intervene in this cycle of violence require heavy staffing so that there is always an adult present to help the children contain their explosive rage; "life-space" or "marginal" interviews (Redl & Wineman, 1951, 1952), which help the children to make connections between their wishes and feelings within the immediacy of the situation; and individual therapy sessions designed to help them understand past abuse and neglect and put the past to rest.

CONCLUSION

Contemporary society presents children with demands for the control of aggressive impulses at a time when wanton aggression seems to pervade daily life. On television and in real life, children are confronted with aggressive acts that challenge their own nascent capacity for controlling aggressive impulses. It is a singular contribution of their report on the war nurseries that Freud and Burlingham were able to trace the impact of violence on the children's efforts to develop controls from within. This work provided a model for understanding the interplay of context and psychological development, which has continuing relevance for study and intervention with contemporary children who are the victims of wanton abuse and neglect.

In their discussion of the war nurseries as a therapeutic milieu, Freud and Burlingham provided a thorough examination of issues that pose problems for residential care and an important guide toward understanding group life more generally in children's treatment centers. Clinical experiences with abused and neglected children in contemporary residential treatment have supported many of the findings of Freud and Burlingham regarding the impact of social violence on child development. Particularly in their descriptions of the aggressive impulses reciprocally evoked in children through daily encounters with violence within the family and community, the reports provide a model for continuing focus on the meanings children make regarding these violent circumstances and the impact of exposure to violence on the child's struggle to manage his or her own urgent wishes to destroy.

Children of violence and despair face an especially arduous task in managing aggressive feelings, and the intensity and urgency of these "primitive and atrocious wishes" (A. Freud, [1941-45] 1973, p. 163) pose particular problems for those responsible for providing care. The account provided by Freud and Burlingham should be supplemented by more specific attention to the response of care givers to the wishes expressed all too often through action by these children of violence. The war nursery reports are relatively silent on the care givers' efforts to resolve their own destructive wishes, including those toward the child. However, the model provided by the reports on the war nurseries and by the more extended discussion of the problems and promises implicit in residential care (Freud & Burlingham, [1944] 1973) provides a wealth of information about providing care for today's children and points to the need for continuing study of the responses of the caretakers.

NOTES

1. James Robertson, then a project social worker, later explored in considerable detail the impact of such transient separations as brief parental hospitalization on the child's mood and sense of personal security (Bowlby et al., 1952).

2. The educational philosophy of the war nurseries was based on the work of August Aichhorn, particularly his *Wayward Youth* (1925), and also on the writings of the pioneering Italian educator Maria Montessori (1870-1952). Young-Bruehl (1988) has provided important information regarding the relationship between Anna Freud and Aichhorn, which began in a joint study group in Vienna and continued through correspondence, particularly following the end of World War II. Her reliance on Montessori's contributions similarly extended back to Vienna and the Burlingham-Rosenfeld School (Ekstein, 1990). Together with the American pragmatist philosopher John Dewey, Montessori was a major influence on the Vienna educational program.

3. Bettelheim (1951, 1960) explicitly warned against the danger that group life would suppress individuality, and he noted the importance of providing a physical environment that is homelike and not uniform and of tailoring the milieu to the needs of individual children. Individualized care and continuing focus on fostering the child's competence would ensure that institutionalization would not be a problem.

4. Data from the World Health Organization cited by Reiss and Roth (1993) show that only the Bahamas and Ecuador, among all the nations of the world, exceeded the United States in homicides per 100,000 population. The United States leads all other nations in sexual assault and is second in the world (following Spain) in robbery. Deaths by homicide rival or exceed casualties in Korea and Vietnam.

5. Gelles and Straus (1987a, 1987b) have reported a recent downward trend in domestic violence, particularly toward children, during the previous decade. This trend is consistent with evidence of reduced levels of violence of all kinds, accompanying the aging of the population. Since much violence is perpetrated by adolescents and young adults, a reduced number of young adults is associated with reduced levels of crime and violence. However, the 1980s was a decade in which social welfare programs were savaged and increasing numbers of people were forced into poverty. It is possible that this increased poverty and the violence associated with "amoral familism" (Banfield, 1958; Stack, 1974) may lead to increased levels of violence over the coming years. Some support for this possibility is evident in figures reported by Aday (1993), which show once again an escalating curve of violence from the mid-1980s to the end of the decade. Aday devotes particular attention to problems of reporting abuse and neglect, which suggests that the violence may be considerably greater than has been assumed and that increased poverty and homelessness have accentuated levels of family violence.

6. In Illinois, a state with an unusually significant welfare caseload, there are at present more than forty thousand children in custody. with one thousand new children added to the rolls each year and a backlog of more than three thousand com-

plaints of abuse and neglect to be investigated. A successful federal suit, brought by the state's Office of the Public Guardian, forced the legislature to provide additional funds. However, there is already a significant deficit in the funds needed to provide services for an ever-growing caseload only a third of the way into 1996.

REFERENCES

Aday, L. (1993). *At Risk in America*: *The Health and Health Care Needs of Vulnerable Populations in the United States*. San Francisco: Jossey-Bass.

Aichhorn, A. (1925). *Wayward Youth* (Trans. E. Bryant, J. Deming, M. O'Neil Hawkins, G. Mohr, E. Mohr, H. Ross, & H. Thun). New York: The Viking Press.

Aichhorn, A. (1964). *Delinquency and Child Guidance*: *Selected Papers*. (Eds. O. Fleischmann, P. Kramer, and H. Ross). New York: International Universities Press (Menninger Clinic Monograph Series No. 15).

Banfield, E. (1958). *The Moral Basis of a Backward Society*. New York: The Free Press.

Beeghly, M., & Cicchetti, D. (1994). Child maltreatment, attachment, and the self system: Emergence of an internal state lexicon in toddlers at high social risk. *Developmental Psychopathology, 6*, 5-30.

Belsky, J. (1980). Child maltreatment: An ecological integration. *American Psychologist, 35*, 320-335.

Belsky, J. (1993). Etiology of child maltreatment: A developmental-ecological analysis. *Psychological Bulletin, 114*, 413-434.

Bettelheim, B. (1943). Mass behavior in an extreme situation. *Journal of Abnormal and Social Psychology, 38*, 417-452.

Bettelheim, B. (1951). *Love Is Not Enough*. New York: Free Press/Macmillan.

Bettelheim, B. (1955). *Truants From Life*. New York: Free Press/Macmillan.

Bettelheim, B. (1960). *The Informed Heart*. New York: The Free Press/Macmillan.

Bettelheim, B. (1967). *The Empty Fortress*. New York: Free Press/Macmillan.

Bowlby, J., Robertson, J., & Rosenbluth, D. (1952). A two-year-old goes to hospital. *Psychoanalytic Study of the Child, 7*, 82-94.

Cicchetti, D., & Barnett, D. (1991). Toward the development of a scientific nosology of child maltreatment. In. D. Cicchetti & W. Grove (Eds.), *Thinking Clearly About Psychology*: *Essays in Honor of Paul E. Meehl*. Minneapolis, MN: The University of Minnesota Press, 346-377.

Cicchetti, D., & Carlson, V. (Eds.). (1989). *Child Maltreatment*: *Theory and Research on the Causes and Consequences of Child Abuse and Neglect*. New York: Cambridge University Press.

Coontz, S. (1992). *The Way We Never Were*: *American Families and the Nostalgia Trap*. New York: Basic Books.

Cummings, E.M., & El-Sheikh, M. (1991). Children's coping with angry environments: A process-oriented approach. In. M. Cummings, A. Greene, & K. Karraker (Eds.), *Life-Span Developmental Psychology*: *Perspectives on Stress and Coping*. Hillsdale, NJ: Lawrence Erlbaum and Associates, 131-150.

Cummings, E.M., Hennesey, K. D., Rabideau, G., & Cicchetti, D. (1994). Responses of physically abused boys to interadult anger involving their mothers. *Developmental Psychopathology, 6*, 31-41.

Demos, J. (1986). *Past, Present and Personal: The Family and the Life Course in American History.* New York: Oxford University Press.

Dodge, K., Bates, J., & Pettit, G. (1990). Mechanisms in the cycle of violence. *Science, 250*, (December 21), 1678-1683.

Downey, G., & Coyne, J. (1990). Children of depressed parents: An integrative review. *Psychological Bulletin, 108*, 50-76.

Eissler, K. (Ed.). (1949). *Searchlights on Delinquency.* Madison, CT: International Universities Press.

Ekstein, R. (1990). Preface to Peter Heller's *A Child Analysis with Anna Freud.* Madison, CT: International Universities Press, ix-xv.

Elson, M. (1986). *Self Psychology in Clinical Social Work.* New York: Norton.

Freud, A. ([1941-1945] 1973). Monthly Reports to the Foster Parents' Plan for War Children, Inc., New York. In. A. Freud, *The Writings of Anna Freud, Volume III: 1939-1945.* New York: International Universities Press, 3-540.

Freud, A. (1972). Comments on aggression. *International Journal of Psychoanalysis, 53*, 163-171.

Freud, A., & Burlingham, D. ([1944]1973). Infants without families: The case for and against residential nurseries. In. A. Freud, *The Writings of Anna Freud, Volume III: 1939-1945.* New York: International Universities Press, 543-664.

Freud, S. ([1913] 1955). The claims of psycho-analysis to scientific interest. In J. Strachey (Ed. and Trans.), *The Standard Edition of the Complete Psychological Works of Sigmund Freud, Vol. 13*, 165-190. London: Hogarth Press.

Freud, S. ([1915] 1955). Instincts and their vicissitudes. In J. Strachey (Ed. and Trans.), *The Standard Edition of the Complete Psychological Works of Sigmund Freud, Vol. 14*, 109-140. London: Hogarth Press.

Freud, S. ([1920] 1955). Beyond the pleasure principle. In J. Strachey (Ed. and Trans.), *The Standard Edition of the Complete Psychological Works of Sigmund Freud (Vol. 18*, pp. 7-66). London: Hogarth Press.

Freud, S. ([1921] 1955). Group psychology and the analysis of the ego. In Strachey (Ed. and Trans.), *The Standard Edition of the Complete Psychological Works of Sigmund Freud (Vol. 18*, pp. 65-144). London: Hogarth Press.

Fromm, E. (1973). *The Anatomy of Human Destructiveness.* New York: Holt, Rinehart and Winston.

Galdston, R. (1981). The domestic dimensions of violence: Child abuse. *Psychoanalytic Study of the Child, 36*, 391-414.

Garbarino, J. (1979). An ecological approach to child maltreatment. In L. Pelton (Ed.), *The Social Context of Child Abuse and Neglect.* New York: Human Sciences Press, 79-102.

Gehrie, M. (1993). Commentary on Marohn's "Rage without content" and Ornstein's "Chronic rage from underground." In. A. Goldberg (Ed.), *The Widening Scope of Self Psychology: Progress in Self-Psychology, Volume 9.* Hillsdale, NJ: The Analytic Press, 159-165.

Gelles, R. (1992). Poverty and violence toward children. *American Behavioral Scientist, 35*, 258-74.

Gelles, R., & Straus, M. (1987a). Is violence toward children increasing? A comparison of 1975 and 1985 national survey rates. *Journal of Interpersonal Violence, 2,* 212-22.

Gelles, R., & Straus, M. (1987b). Is violence toward children increasing? A comparison of 1975 and 1985 national survey rates. In R. Gelles (Ed.), *Family Violence.* Newbury Park, CA: Sage Publications, 78-88.

Gil, D. (1970). *Violence Against Children: Physical Child Abuse in the United States.* Cambridge, MA: Harvard University Press.

Hobbs, N. (1980). Knowledge transfer and the policy process. In G. Gerbner, C.J. Ross, & E. Zigler (Eds.), *Child Abuse: An Agenda for Action.* New York: Oxford University Press, 68-94.

Kaufman, J., & Zigler, E. (1987). Do abused children become abusive parents? *American Journal of Orthopsychiatry, 57,* 186-192.

Kaufman, J., & Zigler, E. (1989). The intergenerational transmission of child abuse. In D. Cicchetti & V. Carlson (Eds.), *Child Maltreatment: Theory and Research on the Causes and Consequence of Child Abuse and Neglect.* New York: Cambridge University Press, 129-150.

Kernberg, O. (1992). *Aggression in Personality Disorders and Perversions.* New Haven, CT: Yale University Press.

Klein, G. (1976). *Psychoanalytic Theory: An Exploration of Essentials.* New York: International Universities Press.

Klein, M. (1948). *Contributions to Psychoanalysis, 1921-1945.* London: Hogarth Press.

Klein, M. ([1932] 1969). *The Psychoanalysis of Children.* London: Hogarth Press.

Klein, M. (1975). *Love, Guilt and Reparation and Other Works, 1927-1945.* New York: Delacorte Press.

Kohut, H. (1959). Introspection, empathy, and psychoanalysis: An examination of the relationship between mode of observation and theory. In P. Ornstein (Ed.), *The Search for the Self, Vol. 1,* New York: International Universities Press, 205-232.

Kohut, H. (1966). Forms and transformations of narcissism. *Journal of the American Psychoanalytic Association, 14*(2), 243-272.

Kohut, H. (1968). The psychoanalytic treatment of narcissistic personality disorders: Outline of a systematic approach. *Psychoanalytic Study of the Child, 23,* 86-113.

Kohut, H. (1971). *The Analysis of the Self.* New York: International Universities Press.

Kohut, H. (1972). Thoughts on narcissism and narcissistic rage. In P. Ornstein (Ed), *The Search for the Self, 2.* New York: International Universities Press, 615-658.

Kohut, H. (1977) *The Restoration of the Self.* New York: International Universities Press.

Kohut, H. ([1981a] 1985). Idealization and cultural self objects. In C. Strozier (Ed.), *Self Psychology and the Humanities: Reflections on a New Psychoanalytic Approach by Heinz Kohut.* New York: Norton, 224-231.

Kohut, H. ([1981b] 1991). (Remarks) On Empathy. In. H. Kohut, *Search for the Self: Selected Writings of Heinz Kohut: 1978-1981.* (Ed.) P. H. Ornstein. New York: International Universities Press, 4, 525-536.

Kohut, H. (1982). Introspection, empathy, and the semi-circle of mental health, *International Journal of Psychoanalysis, 63,* 395-407.

Kohut, H. (1984). *How Does Psychoanalysis Cure?* Chicago: The University of Chicago Press.

Kohut, H. (1985). *Self Psychology and the Humanities: Reflections on a New Psychoanalytic Approach.* C. Strozier (Ed.). New York: Norton.

Kohut, H., & Wolf, E. (1978). The disorders of the self and their treatment: An outline. *International Journal of Psychoanalysis, 59,* 413-425.

Lewin, K. (1951). *Field Theory in Social Science.* (Ed. D. Cartwright). New York: Harper and Row.

Lore, R., & Schultz, L. (1993). Control of human aggression: A comparative perspective, *American Psychologist, 48,* 16-25.

Marohn, R. (1993). Rage without content. In A. Goldberg (Ed.), *The Widening Scope of Self Psychology: Progress in Self-Psychology.* Hillsdale, NJ: The Analytic Press, *9,* 129-141.

Massey, D., & Denton, N. (1993). *American Apartheid: Segregation and the Making of the Underclass.* Cambridge, MA: Harvard University Press.

Minturn, L., & Lambert, W. (1964). *Mothers of six cultures: Antecedents of childrearing.* New York: Wiley.

National Research Council. (1990). *Who Cares for America's Children.* Washington, DC: National Academy Press.

National Research Council. (1993). *Understanding Child Abuse and Neglect.* (Panel on Research on Child Abuse and Neglect). Washington, DC: National Academy Press.

Ornstein, P. (1993). Chronic rage from underground: Reflections on its structure and treatment. In A. Goldberg (Ed.), *The Widening Scope of Self Psychology: Progress in Self-Psychology.* Hillsdale, NJ: The Analytic Press, *9,* 129-141.

Patterson, G.R. (1982). *Coercive Family Processes.* Eugene, OR: Castalia Publishing Company.

Pavenstedt, E. (Ed.). (1967). *The Drifters: Children of Disorganized Lower-Class Families.* Boston: Little-Brown.

Rank, B. (1949). Aggression. *Psychoanalytic Study of the Child, 3/4,* 43-48.

Redl, F., & Wineman, D. (1951). *Children Who Hate: The Disorganization and Breakdown of Behavior Controls.* New York: Free Press/Macmillan.

Redl, F., & Wineman, D. (1952). *Controls from Within: Techniques for the Treatment of the Aggressive Child.* New York: The Free Press/Macmillan.

Reiss, A., Jr., & Roth, J. (1993). (Eds.) *Understanding and Preventing Violence.* Washington, DC: National Academy Press.

Schmideberg, M. (1949). The analytic treatment of major criminals: Therapeutic results and technical problems. In Eissler, K. (Ed.), *Searchlights on Delinquency.* New York: International Universities Press, 174-189.

Sedlak, A.J. ([1988] 1991). *National Incidence and Prevalence of Child Abuse and Neglect.* Rockville, MD: Westat Publishing Company.

Solnit, A. (1994). A psychoanalytic view of child abuse. In Sugarman, A. (Ed.), *Victims of Abuse: The Emotional Impact of Child and Adult Trauma.* Madison, CT: International Universities Press, 25-44.

Stack, C. (1974). *All Our Kin*: *Strategies for Survival in a Black Community*. New York: Harper Torchbooks.

Stone, L. (1971). Reflections on the psychoanalytic concept of aggression. *Psychoanalytic Quarterly, XL*, 195-244.

Strauss, M., & Gelles, R. (1990). *Physical Violence in American Families*: *Risk Factors and Adaptation to Violence in 8145 Families*. New Brunswick, NJ: Transactions Publishers.

Straus, M., Gelles, R., & Steinmetz, S.K. (1980). *Behind Closed Doors*: *Violence in the American Family*. Garden City, NY: Doubleday/Anchor Books.

Sugarman, A. (1994). Trauma and abuse: An overview. In A. Sugarman (Ed.), *Victims of Abuse*: *The Emotional Impact of Child and Adult Trauma*. Madison, CT: International Universities Press, 1-24.

Terman, D. (1975). Aggression and narcissistic rage: A clinical elaboration. *The Annual of Psychoanalysis, 3*, 239-255.

Trickett, P., & Putnam, F. (1994). The impact of child sexual abuse upon females: Toward a developmental psychobiological integration. *Psychological Science, 4*(2), 81-87.

Whiting, B. (Ed.). (1963). *Six Cultures*: *Studies of Childrearing*. New York: Wiley.

Wilson, W. J. (1987). *The Truly Disadvantaged: The Inner City, The Underclass, and Public Policy*. Chicago: the University of Chicago Press.

Wilson, W. J. (Ed.). (1989). *The Ghetto Underclass*: *Social Science Perspectives*. Newbury Park, CA: Sage Publications.

Winnicott, D. W. ([1936,1964] 1984). Aggression and its roots. In D. W. Winnicott, *Deprivation and Delinquency* (C. Winnicott, R. Shepard, & M. Davis, Eds.). London: Routledge, 81-99.

Winnicott, D. W. ([1940] 1984). Children in the war. In D. W. Winnicott, *Deprivation and Delinquency* (C. Winnicott, R. Shepard, & M. Davis, Eds.). London: Routledge, 25-30.

Winnicott, D. W. ([1947] 1984). Residential management as treatment for difficult children. In D. W. Winnicott, *Deprivation and Delinquency* (C. Winnicott, R. Shepard, & M. Davis, Eds.). London: Routledge, 54-72.

Winnicott, D. W. (1953). Transitional objects and transitional phenomena. In D. W. Winnicott, *Collected Papers*: *Through Pediatrics to Psychoanalysis*. New York: Basic Books, 229-242.

Winnicott, D. W. (1960a). The theory of the parent-infant relationship. *International Journal of Psychoanalysis, 41*, 585-595.

Winnicott, D. W. ([1960b] 1984). Aggression, guilt and reparation. In D. W. Winnicott, *Deprivation and Delinquency* (C. Winnicott, R. Shepard, & M. Davis, Eds.). London: Routledge, 145-155.

Winnicott, D. W. (1984). *Deprivation and Delinquency*. C. Winnicott, R. Shepard, and M. Davis (Eds.). London: Routledge.

Winnicott, D. W. (1988). *Human Nature*. New York: Schocken Books.

Wolf, E. (1988). *Treating the Self*: *Elements of Clinical Self Psychology*. New York: Guilford Press.

Young-Bruehl, E. (1988). *Anna Freud*: *A Biography*. New York: Summit.

Zigler, E., & Hall, N. (1989). Physical child abuse in America: Past, present, and future. In D. Cicchetti & V. Carlson (Eds.), *Child Maltreatment: Theory and Research on the Causes and Consequence of Child Abuse and Neglect*. New York: Cambridge University Press, 38-75.

BIOGRAPHICAL NOTES

Bertram J. Cohler, PhD, is William Rainey Harper Professor of Social Sciences, the College and the Departments of Psychology (Committee on Human Development), Psychiatry, and Education, University of Chicago, and a faculty member, Chicago Institute for Psychoanalysis.

D. Patrick Zimmerman, PsyD, is Lecturer, the Department of Psychiatry, University of Chicago, a member of the Senior Associate Core Faculty at the Illinois School of Professional Psychology/Chicago, Coordinator of Research, the Sonia Shankman Orthogenic School, and a graduate of the Center for Psychoanalysis.

From Disciplinary Control to Benign Milieu in Children's Residential Treatment

D. Patrick Zimmerman, PsyD
Bertram J. Cohler, PhD

SUMMARY. This discussion of group and individual aspects of residential treatment begins with an examination of the historical development of residential care and the concept of the therapeutic milieu in the United States. The historical review then turns to a consideration of some of the more recent advances made in our understanding of theories about treatment. Given the evolvement of contemporary theories, the paper discusses a number of selected difficulties which remain embedded in current discussions about group care, including: (1) the sometimes conflicting assumptions of a medical model of treatment versus milieu therapy; (2) efforts to define an appropriate psychological model to adequately describe milieu therapy or the therapeutic community; and (3) the potentially inherent conflict between the assumptions of individual psychotherapy and milieu therapy, when both are provided within the context of residential group care. *[Article copies available for a fee from The Haworth Document Delivery Service: 1-800-342-9678. E-mail address: <getinfo@haworthpressinc.com> Website: <http://www.HaworthPress.com>]*

KEYWORDS. Residential treatment, milieu therapy, Fritz Redl, Bruno Bettelheim, child psychotherapy

An earlier version of this article was published in *Therapeutic Communities: The International Journal for Therapeutic & Supportive Communities*, 19(2), 123-146, 1998.

[Haworth co-indexing entry note]: "From Disciplinary Control to Benign Milieu in Children's Residential Treatment." Zimmerman, D. Patrick, and Bertram J. Cohler. Co-published simultaneously in *Residential Treatment for Children & Youth* (The Haworth Press, Inc.) Vol. 18, No. 2, 2000, pp. 27-54; and: *The Forsaken Child: Essays on Group Care and Individual Therapy* (D. Patrick Zimmerman) The Haworth Press, Inc., 2000, pp. 27-54. Single or multiple copies of this article are available for a fee from The Haworth Document Delivery Service [1-800-342-9678, 9:00 a.m. - 5:00 p.m. (EST). E-mail address: getinfo@haworthpressinc.com].

27

INTRODUCTION:
THE PROMISE OF GROUP CARE
FOR CHILDREN OF ABUSE AND NEGLECT

In a time of concern with managed care and reduced lengths of treatment for troubled children and adolescents in the United States, we are confronted ironically with an ever larger number of children, most often those born in circumstances of urban social disorganization and personal despair, who are unable to profit from traditional modes of intervention and were portrayed so well by Redl and Wineman (1951, 1952) as the children no one wants. Psychologically damaged from earliest childhood, these children have been described as throwaway children; too many professionals in the field of child welfare have concluded that these children suffer from primary attachment disorders and are unable to respond to remediation. Often unable to respond to short-term treatment approaches, they sometimes become incorrigible adults with often horrible criminal outcomes. The perspective provided in this study provides an alternative. More than half a century of study and intervention with these children has shown that a focus on the interplay between the child and the group within a setting that "smiles," and in which all aspects of the child's daily life have been organized in order to facilitate mastery and growth, is sometimes able to provide the conditions which are necessary for these children to realize sustained psychological development, including the emergence of strengthened ego controls and an enhanced sense of personal integrity.

This discussion of group and individual aspects of residential treatment involves an examination of the historical development of residential care and the concept of the therapeutic milieu in the United States. This turning to the past is compelled by more than simple nostalgia or a romantic antiquarianism. Rather, it can lead to a reconsideration of many of the persisting dilemmas which even today confront our efforts to provide milieu therapy within residential treatment. Some of the difficulties which remain embedded in contemporary discussions about group care include: (1) the sometimes conflicting assumptions of a medical model of treatment versus milieu therapy or the therapeutic community; (2) efforts to define an appropriate psychological model to adequately describe milieu therapy or the therapeutic community; and (3) the potentially inherent conflict between the assumptions of individual psychotherapy and milieu therapy, when both are provided within the context of residential group care.

Many of the authors' views about residential care have been influenced by their associations with the Sonia Shankman Orthogenic School at the University of Chicago. Therefore, a brief summary of the school's development over time is useful in providing the reader with some context for the views on group and individual treatment in residential care presented in this paper. The Orthogenic School was originally established in 1912 as a clinic affiliated with Rush Medical College in Chicago, and its original aims were the "mental examination of children with 'doubtful mentality'" and the instruction of medical students who "would almost inevitably find the feeble minded in their practice" (Young, 1938). For many years, the school was viewed primarily as a research center, and the earliest available descriptions of the student population tended to be quite limited and focused upon intelligence measures. One of the most valuable research findings of the school during this era was that children's I.Q.'s were not fixed, but could increase with appropriate educational interventions (Jenuwine, 1990). After the Orthogenic School's formal 1930 affiliation with the University of Chicago, the school began to work with children who displayed reading disabilities and behavior disorders, as well as with mentally deficient youth.

Bruno Bettelheim became Principal of the school in 1944, and within three years the diagnostic population had shifted to one described as mostly composed of young "delinquent" types and children with psychosomatic disturbances, with no students scoring in the retarded or borderline-retarded ranges of intelligence. From the 1950s until Bettelheim's retirement in 1972, the school focussed its work primarily upon children with schizophrenic disorders, with a small subgroup of children diagnosed as autistic (Zimmerman, 1994). While much of this paper will discuss Bettelheim's contributions to the development of theories about group care for children with these severe disorders, the authors are quite aware of the many accusations which have arisen about Dr. Bettelheim's actual practices subsequent to his death. However, it is beyond the scope of this study to address that controversy, and interested readers are referred to the authors' detailed examinations of that debate, which have appeared elsewhere (Cohler, 1996; Zimmerman, 1997a, b).

The Orthogenic School is presently located on the University of Chicago campus, in an urban residential neighborhood. The school is coeducational and presently has a capacity of 40 children and adolescents. The average residency during the 1980s was 5.6 years, although in recent years the length of stay has decreased somewhat. The school's current student population has treatment characteristics which are similar to groups described elsewhere as difficult to treat, or treatment resistant (McGlashan, 1984; Gossett, Lewis, & Barnhart, 1983). Since the 1980s, behavior disorders, sometimes in conjunction with borderline or schizophrenic disturbances, have become more prevalent. Further, today's students frequently have no financial or family resources. The prevalence of severe child maltreatment, lower socioeconomic status, and a higher prevalence of minority racial or ethnic backgrounds, all combine to present a strikingly different demographic picture from the one which described students at the Orthogenic School during Bettelheim's tenure. With rare exceptions, the disturbances seem to be of early origin and long duration; most students have had earlier outpatient individual psychotherapy, prior inpatient psychiatric hospitalizations, or both. Having experienced such abuse and neglect, these young people experience an enfeebled sense of self, find it difficult to modulate even the most fleeting disappointment or momentary failures of empathy on the part of the devoted staff of mental health professionals working with these children in the classroom, dormitory, or individual sessions. Cooper (1986) and Sugarman (1994) have well summarized the impact of early life trauma upon the lives of these children and the means which children use in the effort to overcome the impact of traumatic experiences early in life. Early abuse and neglect have been compounded by the wages of neglect over periods often a decade or longer, as these children are shifted from foster home to institutional setting and as their enfeebled sense of self struggles against overwhelming odds.

The so-called disruptive behavior disorders, such as conduct disorder or oppositional disorder, well described in the child psychiatry literature (Dishion, French, & Patterson, 1995) reflect a response to a world experienced as unreliable and overwhelming. One form of group or milieu intervention consists of providing a degree of reliability and constancy previously not experienced by these children, with an explicit focus on supporting an enfeebled self through the provision of a corrective emotional experience in which mental health professionals work with their own affects, counter to those of the children, in order to tolerate the children's disappointments. Those disappointments are often reflected in disruptive action, which can be offset by staff efforts at an enhanced, empathic appreciation of the terrors which so often underlay these children's rageful outbursts, and which so often color their ongoing experiences of the details of everyday life. This empathic attunement can be supplemented by carefully tailored positive reinforcements for students' efforts to strive for new, more adaptive outcomes to present-day conflicts and problems reflecting old traumatic themes.

The basic treatment approach of the school was for many years a psychoanalytically-informed one; recently, more behaviorally-oriented techniques have been introduced to augment the milieu setting. There is an emphasis on an interdisciplinary treatment staff, which is composed of dormitory counselors, special education staff, individual psychotherapists, a clinical director, an executive director, and outside clinical consultants. At the core of the school's approach is a strong emphasis on a psychotherapeutic treatment milieu. Continued educational growth is encouraged for the staff members at the school. For example, all of the full-time dormitory counselors and classroom teaching assistants are offered university coursework, the completion of which can lead to a clinically-oriented graduate degree from the university.

EARLY FOUNDATIONS OF MILIEU THERAPY IN THE UNITED STATES

Hoffman and Singer (1977) noted that the classical works they reviewed in the field of milieu therapy or the therapeutic community suggested that most, if not all, of the early studies in this area were based upon work and research undertaken at inpatient hospital settings. Nevertheless, there have been *many* threads in the historical development of the concept of milieu therapy, and one of the most direct lines of theory contribution occurred within the field of residential care, as distinguished from hospital settings. In the United States, some of the initial efforts to develop and implement the concept of milieu treatment included important clinical work done at two innovative residential treatment programs for children and adolescents, through the collaboration between Bruno Bettelheim at the University of Chicago, and Fritz Redl and David Wineman at Wayne State University. Over the course of the period immediately following the Second World War, these collaborators made major contributions to the development of the concept of milieu as a therapeutic modality in the United States: by Bettelheim at the Sonia Shankman Orthogenic School of The University of Chicago, and by Redl and Wineman first at Pioneer House in Detroit and later by Redl on the children's inpatient unit at The National Institutes of Mental Health in Bethesda, Maryland.

The efforts of Bettelheim, Redl and Wineman were similarly influenced by the integration of psychoanalysis and pedagogy first reported by Aichhorn (1925) in his work with delinquent adolescents in Austria, as well as by the work in the war nurseries reported by Anna Freud and Dorothy Burlingham (Freud, [1941-45] 1973; Freud & Burlingham, [1944], 1973; Cohler & Zimmerman, 1997) with children removed from their families during the bombing of London in the Second World War. The implementation of the concept of milieu by Redl, Wineman, and Bettelheim, extending the thoughts and observations of Aichhorn and Anna Freud, was in large part a function of particular concerns about working with troubled children and adolescents in urban areas of the United States. This collaborative effort was extended by the contributions of other colleagues, including Fritz Mayer at the Bellefaire School in Cleveland, Ohio, and Rudolph Ekstein at the Southard School of the Menninger Clinic in Topeka, Kansas.

Bettelheim's interest in the impact of environment was first inspired by his experiences in the Nazi concentration camps for political prisoners in the late 1930s, while Redl and Wineman's work was influenced in important respects by the research of Kurt Lewin ([1941] 1951; [1943] 1951; [1944] 1951; [1947] 1951) and his colleagues at The University of Michigan's Research Center for Group Dynamics. Bettelheim's focus was principally on the impact of the environment in fostering the sense of individuality. Having experienced the manner in which the experienced environment could contribute to the destruction of personality in the concentration camps, his concern was initially with the role of the environment in promoting a capacity for mastery and a sense of integrity. Redl and Wineman and, subsequently, Gisele Knopka at The University of Minnesota, focused particularly on the use of the group and group process, together with therapeutic programming, as a vehicle for personal change. Group decision making, as well as the role of the child within this process, was highlighted in Redl and Wineman's work.

This milieu perspective experienced great popularity during the first two decades after the Second World War, with a number of other children's centers taking advantage of the humanistic perspective provided by the milieu approach (Trieschman, Whittaker, & Brendtro, 1969). In addition to the psychodynamic milieu approach, a number of other types of group care treatment approaches for troubled youth were developed subsequent to the early pioneering psychoanalytically-informed work in the United States (Zimmerman, 1990). Some of those developments included perspectives represented by the "positive peer culture" model (Brendtro & Wasmund, 1989), behavioral therapy (Blase, Fixsen, Freeborn, & Jaeger, 1989), and Hobbs' residential psychoeducational approach at the Re-Ed schools (Lewis & Lewis, 1989).

In recent times, behavioral methodologies have become a major challenge to the influence of psychodynamic approaches in many milieu aspects of residential treatment in the United States. Nevertheless, Redl and Wineman's approach to the life-space or marginal interview has survived and even become the premier method for crisis management in children's daily living experiences within many institutions. For example, techniques developed by the Therapeutic Crisis Intervention project at Cornell University (Family Life Development Center, 1993), used widely within children's centers nationwide, are explicitly based upon the set of techniques described by Redl and Wineman (1952) for the "antiseptic" manipulation of surface behavior and for the clinical exploitation of life events. Perhaps more important than the survival of psychodynamically-oriented management techniques, the value of Aichhorn's findings about the importance of early personal attachments and of Anna Freud's war nursery observation's of children's reactions to separations from maternal figures has been reflected in the large body of subsequent literature about the nature of the child-caregiver tie and attachment theory (Cohler & Zimmerman, 1996) and a renewed interest in the use of techniques based upon attachment theory in inpatient and residential treatment settings (Adam, Keller, Sheldon, & West, 1995; Fritsch & Goodrich, 1990; Small, Kennedy, & Bender, 1991; Swanson & Schaefer, 1988; Zimmerman, 1993). This revival of interest in attachment issues has been stimulated by the substantial increase in the numbers of abused and neglected children being referred for group care, and by the need to develop or refine treatment responses which can be benign and understanding of the particular terrors and rages often displayed by those children.

BETTELHEIM'S CONCEPT
OF THE "THERAPEUTIC MILIEU"

Theoretical Contributions

Reflecting on the power of the concentration camp to change personality, Bettelheim (1943, 1960) recognized the power of the total environment to change behavior for good or ill. The concept of the total environment included both the interpersonal world and the physical environment in which intervention took place. Aware of the often numbing impact of institutional life upon the personality, Bettelheim created a series of physical spaces linked by common themes, but distinctive and likely to assist children in maintaining contact with the world (Bettelheim, 1974). For example, since the children at the school, as with so many "normal" children, experienced difficulty shifting from one activity to another, such as working on a model in the dormitory and then having to stop with the advent of suppertime, stairway and halls were well lit and colorfully decorated. Beyond that, Bettelheim also focused on issues of group life, creating dormitories with six or seven distinctive beds and dressers, and a group table whose dimensions were worked out by Bettelheim as ideal for the number of children enrolled.

As already noted, Bettelheim's early writings regarding the treatment of disturbed children appear to have been deeply influenced by his dialogues with a small group of immigrant psychoanalytic clinicians from Vienna and Anna Freud's circle, which included Fritz Redl and his colleague from his work in Detroit, David Wineman (Ekstein, 1990). Bettelheim also communicated extensively with Rudolph Ekstein (The Menninger Clinic) and his colleague at the Orthogenic School, the Chicago psychoanalyst Emmy Sylvester. Bettelheim's clinical writings appeared somewhat later than the political ones, for which he had initially achieved notoriety. Much of Bettelheim's early work focused on attempts to define and further develop the concept of milieu therapy and, in particular, to describe from a theoretical perspective its early implementation and use with emotionally disturbed children at the Orthogenic School (Bettelheim, 1948a,b, 1949; Bettelheim & Sylvester, 1947, 1948, 1949a,b, 1950). Although this focus on the concept and clinical importance of the milieu was central throughout Bettelheim's body of clinical writing, it can be argued that a fully systematic, structured presentation of his understanding of the practical details of the milieu at the Orthogenic School did not appear until the publication of *A Home for the Heart* (1974), more than twenty-five years after publishing his first article about milieu therapy.

In his early clinical writings, Bettelheim acknowledged that milieu therapy was not a new psychotherapeutic technique. He knew that Anna Freud had earlier considered issues of residential treatment, although with skepticism, as a possible adjunct for child analysis with children suffering from the more severe psychopathological disorders (A. Freud, 1954). As noted earlier, Bettelheim was also familiar with August Aichhorn's efforts to realize the therapeutic potential of a carefully arranged institutional setting at a correctional facility for adolescents. Further, at the time that Bettelheim was beginning to develop his clinical ideas at the Orthogenic School, he was quite interested in and well-informed about the work of Fritz Redl, who was already engaged in the use of special milieu therapy techniques with disturbed children at the Pioneer House experiment in Detroit, and who had begun publishing his findings some time before Bettelheim's first clinical treatment efforts (Redl, 1942, 1943, 1944, 1949). A major emphasis in Redl's writings was on developing for staff members methods of behavioral control, techniques for therapeutic interview interventions in the milieu, and strategies for maintaining the structure or framework of the milieu. At the Orthogenic School, however, the structure or framework of the milieu was assumed–it rested significantly upon the authoritative presence of Bettelheim as the director of the school.

One might characterize Aichhorn's perspective as largely an effort to apply Freudian psychoanalytic drive theory to reconstructively understand delinquent symptoms and to prescribe treatment techniques (specifically the promotion and use of the positive transference), within a total environment for delinquent adolescents. Much of his writing about work with those youth had a focus on understanding the genetic psychodynamics of the *individual* within the context of the larger setting. Redl's focus, on the other hand, was much more on the techniques for *management of group process* (including the elaboration of the concept of the "life-space interview") and understanding the effects of the group upon the individual. Somewhat differently, many of Bettelheim's writings about the milieu were largely concerned with describing the rationale, structure, and effects of an *already existent* cohesive, well organized, yet organizationally simple, therapeutic environment on the emotional process of rehabilitation. His work tended to emphasize anecdotal illustrations from highly detailed psychodynamic case material of individual students, rather than on the specification of practical strategies or techniques for maintaining the stability of a therapeutic setting.

As with Redl, Bettelheim's clinical descriptions were often stated in terms of ego psychology, in contrast to Aichhorn's more classical Freudian drive model. On the other hand, Bettelheim and Redl tended to emphasize different ego psychology perspectives, although at times each shared the viewpoint of the other to some extent. In terms of differences, Redl more often stressed the defensive aspect of ego functioning, and portrayed the ego as a psychic structure fundamentally in battle against the drives. From this *conflict* perspective, Redl's focus was upon the *defenses* of the ego, which for the delinquent were either too weak, or were in collusion with the demands of the impulses for immediate gratification, against the demands of reality or the conscience. Bettelheim, on the other hand, tended to view the ego from the *deficit* perspective, as underdeveloped and too often *lacking* in the development of even primitive defenses against impulse discharge. As a result, his theories about treatment more directly emphasized the *adaptive* aspects of the ego, and specifically the need to carefully structure and dose environmental stimuli so as to enable the ego's adaptive strivings. Thus, while Redl's writings often stressed the development of techniques for staff members to actively confront residents' inadequate defensive structures, Bettelheim stressed the potential growth-promoting capacities of the milieu's overall detailed structure, characterized by carefully measured exposure to the demands of external reality, without (in theory) a reliance upon approaches which directly confronted children's failures of or disturbances in ego function.

Despite the variations just noted, it is clear that Bettelheim shared in the tradition of the work done by Aichhorn and Redl, reflected in part by his early initial interest in the treatment of delinquent youth and his belief in the potentially beneficial effects of milieu treatment for them (Bettelheim, 1955; Bettelheim & Sylvester, 1949a,b, 1950). In this context, Bettelheim's early writings about milieu therapy addressed the delinquent's concern for and confusion about moral issues (Bettelheim & Sylvester, 1950), somatic symptoms which develop in children as they begin to give up their delinquent, tension discharging patterns of behavior (Bettelheim, 1948b; Bettelheim & Sylvester, 1949b), and the appropriateness of open versus closed treatment institutions for delinquents (Bettelheim, 1948a). The latter discussion represented Bettelheim's attempt to cope with a difference in treatment perspectives with which clinicians continue to struggle today, specifically between assumptions derived from the medical model of treatment and the precepts of milieu therapy or the therapeutic community. This tension was further elaborated by Jules Henry, a cultural anthropologist, in his studies of the organization of the Orthogenic School, as contrasted with hospital in-patient facilities (Henry, 1954, 1957a,b). Henry's observations were later incorporated into Bettelheim's (1974) discussion of the differences between the organizational structures and dynamics of a traditional mental hospital (a medical model) from those at the Orthogenic School (a milieu model).

Over the succeeding time of study and work with these children, Bettelheim gradually shifted the major thrust of his writings away from delinquency, and he began to concentrate more particularly on the attempt to describe the etiology and the milieu treatment of schizophrenic children. The underlying, paradoxical connection between Bettelheim's conception of the therapeutic milieu and the German concentration camp experiences was vividly illustrated in one of his most widely-read early articles on childhood schizophrenia, "Schizophrenia as a Reaction to Extreme Situations" (Bettelheim, 1956), the title of which was, of course, only a slight variation of the title of his original commentary on the disintegrative psychological effects of the Nazi concentration camps (1943). In that 1956 paper, Bettelheim asserted his belief that an important similarity between the two situations was "that the youngster who develops childhood schizophrenia seems to feel about himself and his life exactly as the concentration camp prisoner felt about his, namely, that he is totally at the mercy of irrational forces which are bent on using him for their goals, irrespective of his" (Bettelheim, 1956, p. 512). Thus, Bettelheim claimed, "the psychological cause of childhood schizophrenia is the child's subjective feeling of living permanently in an extreme situation . . . helpless in the face of threats to his very life, at the mercy of insensitive powers which are motivated only by their own incomprehensible whims, and of being deprived of any interpersonal, need-satisfying relationship" (Bettelheim, 1956, p. 513). This stance, as well as his strident manner of presenting it, unfortunately led to Bettelheim's later widespread reputation for blaming parents for their children's disturbances, as well as to his practice of enforcing prolonged separations of children from their families.

Further, Bettelheim felt that there was another strong parallel between what he interpreted to be the schizophrenic reactions among the fellow prisoners he had observed during his own internment and the symptoms associated with autism and schizophrenia in children being referred to the Orthogenic School. In particular, both the psychological devastation precipitated by the concentration camp experience and the symptomatology of childhood schizophrenia appeared to be, for Bettelheim, the consequence of a massive regression (Bettelheim, 1956). Bettelheim's reflections about his observations of camp prisoners' experiences led him to hypothesize that a milieu constructed as the *opposite* of the camp environment could facilitate significant psychological rehabilitation, pointing out another author's speculation that "if one has seen how the prisoners experienced utter deterioration when exposed to such conditions and how quickly they regain their human qualities after liberation, once they feel assured of relative security and adequate food, one gains some inkling of what a world could be like in which every human being had absolute assurance that his life and needs would be guaranteed by the social structure instead of being endangered by it" (Bettelheim, 1947, p. 637).

In general, Bettelheim's initial writings attempted to specify some of the beneficial group effects of milieu treatment upon the individual child (Bettelheim & Sylvester, 1947), to describe some of the general characteristics of and indications for milieu treatment (Bettelheim & Sylvester, 1948, 1949a), and to distinguish between a therapeutic "home," a psychiatric treatment center, and a "psychiatric school" (Bettelheim, 1949). With regard to the over-riding characteristics of a therapeutic milieu, Bettelheim repeatedly emphasized the need, applied in ways particular to each child, for an almost *unconditional gratification* of the child's basic needs, a secure and protective setting, and *carefully measured dosages of reality*. More specifically, in Bettelheim's early efforts to outline his understanding of the concept of milieu, he appears to have attempted to define milieu therapy from three major vantage points: (1) the type of patient most appropriate for residential milieu care, (2) the distinctions between traditional psychotherapy and milieu therapy, and (3) the proper temporal focus of milieu therapy.

Theoretical Dilemmas

Despite Bettelheim's many efforts to elaborate a theory of milieu treatment and to implement a therapeutic milieu at the Orthogenic School, his writings also point to a number of seemingly diametrically opposed perspectives, to difficult issues with which clinicians in this area of work still struggle today. The following theoretical dilemmas, and there are assuredly many more, are presented not as a critique of any particular position, but rather as issues of which we must have an ongoing *awareness*, and about which we must often devote considerable thought. In terms of Bettelheim's writings about the milieu, he often ended up giving us a richly detailed picture of the physical structure and routines of the environment. From this vantage point, it was difficult to pinpoint anything which had treatment *specificity*, because it seemed that *every detail* of the milieu had equal valence in terms of treatment impact. Again, Bettelheim's discussions of the milieu, although sometimes clinical in a general or rhetorical way, were not really psychological presentations, except in terms of rather static ego-psychology terminology (e.g., strengthening "ego" controls, carefully dosing reality experiences).

This raises the issue of the importance of going beyond one-person psychological conceptualizations in our understanding of the milieu treatment modality. The discussion of one- versus two-person models of psychology has become an issue of fundamental concern in recent years. There have been important shifts in our understanding of psychoanalytic theory and technique, movements from a loyalist adherence to the classical objectivist, one-person analytic model, to the contemporary efforts to refine the two-person and, further, social-constructivist perspective of psychoanalysis. While it is well beyond the scope of this paper to fully discuss the shift away from the one-person model, different characteristics of that shift have been elaborated in a number of important contemporary works (Altman, 1993, 1995; Bollas, 1987; Ehrenberg, 1992; Gill, 1994; Hoffman, 1994: Levenson, 1983; Mitchell, 1988, 1997; Ogden, 1986; Racker, 1968; Searles, 1965; Stolorow & Atwood, 1992; Tansey & Burke, 1989). The classical, one-person model of psychology has been characterized by an adherence to a number of positions, including: (1) an exclusively inner or intrapsychic focus in treatment; (2) loyalty to one or another intrapsychic, one-person model of development (drive, ego, and some earlier forms of self and relational psychology); (3) adherence to the myth of therapist "neutrality"; (4) an over-riding view of the patient as sick and subordinate to the therapist in the treatment relationship; (5) characterization of the patient's perceptions of the therapist as "transference distortions"; (6) emphasis upon therapist abstinence, as opposed to the provision of support, suggestion, and direction; (7) the almost exclusive focus upon the past, with efforts to reconstruct or uncover the "truths" of the past; and (8) a belief that insight is the mutative factor in treatment.

On the other hand, the two-person model of psychology acknowledges the importance of the external world and interpersonal experiences, while emphasizing relational developmental models. It acknowledges and values the therapist's real, personal involvement in the treatment setting, and it accepts that patients' reactions are not necessarily pathological distortions. As a corollary to this view, there has been a movement away from viewing the therapist's countertransference as a malignant, avoidable intrusion into the treatment process, toward an appreciation of it as an ongoing current with a valuable purpose (Racker, 1968; Gill, 1994; Hoffman, 1992, 1994; Mitchell, 1997). This view of countertransference as potentially leading to an enhanced understanding of patients, and opening up new treatment potentials in the process, has been acknowledged in residential treatment for some time (Borowitz, 1970; Bleiberg, 1987). Further, there is a more open awareness and acceptance of therapists' influences in terms of support, suggestion, and direction, along with a more positive assessment of those actions. Finally, rather than limiting the therapist's stance to one of abstinence and interpretation, a two-person psychology stance views therapeutic relational *experience* and the creation of meaning in that relationship (rather than the *discovery* of truths from the past) as the more important mutative factors.

More recently, the constructivist position has argued for going beyond the one-person/two-person treatment dichotomy. For example, Hoffman (1998) argues against viewing one-person versus two-person psychologies as necessary polarities. Instead, he proposes the need for understanding *both* social and individual perspectives as they emerge in the treatment process, in a dialectical, figure-ground interplay enabling the potential for a synthesis of the two perspectives. By this, Hoffman means that the two perspectives are interdependent and together form a whole, but a whole which can only be described in terms of the figure-ground interaction. Further, for each of the perspectives, inside the understanding of one, there are parts of the other; neither position is without features of the other.

Hoffman's recent writings (1994, 1998), have shifted the major focus from the elaboration of distinctions between the objectivist and constructivist perspectives, to an emphasis upon and exploration of a dialectical way of thinking about psychoanalytic theory and the analyst's participation in the treatment process. From the perspective of dialectical thinking, according to Hoffman, it becomes apparent that *many* psychoanalytic concepts imply dichotomous ways of thinking, rather than an integrative approach to seeming polarities. These seemingly opposing conceptual views include: "[fantasy] versus reality, repetition versus new experience, self-expression versus responsivity to others, technique versus personal relationship, interpretation versus enactment, individual versus social, intrapsychic versus interpersonal, construction versus discovery, even analyst versus patient" (Hoffman, 1994, p. 195). In Hoffman's later discussions (1998) of this perspective, he argues for the potentially liberating effects of a dialectical way of thinking, while examining the seemingly "chimerical" polarities of loyalist adherence to the analytic frame versus "deviations" from the frame, the stance of personal expressiveness versus technical principles and a "diagnostic" focus, and the "liminal" analytic space which can exist between "spontaneous, egalitarian relatedness" versus "structured, hierarchical role-relatedness." For Hoffman, the integrative, dialectical approach to these seeming dichotomies entails always viewing them in figure-ground relationships, rather than as simply mutually exclusive polarities.

Although Bettelheim knew well that the milieu was primarily an interpersonal field (requiring at least a two-person psychological theory), his writings which focused more exclusively upon the milieu tended to be from the one-person psychological perspective of his time. Further, Bettelheim's case study reconstructions, for which he is probably best known as a clinical thinker, were almost exclusively examples of one-person psychologies (based upon either classical drive theory or ego psychology formulations), although there was some evidence that his later thinking was beginning to shift toward a two-person, more interpersonal model of treatment (Bettelheim, 1967, pp. 3-49). This tendency to describe what is intrinsically an interpersonal setting from a one-person psychology stance persists in much of the writing today about milieu therapy. This is complicated even more by the increased use of medications and of behavioral techniques in today's residential treatment settings. The former is, of course, associated with many aspects of the one-person medical model (Hoffman & Singer, 1977), while the latter could be viewed metaphorically as the one-person "medical model" of present-day psychology, with its emphasis upon directly observable results and learning through the application of contingencies. Both medical and behavioral models share precepts associated with a reliance upon empirical proof and an optimism in technological advance. On the other hand, the assumptions of two-person individual psychotherapy, milieu therapy and the therapeutic community are based more within the realm of the interpersonal. With regard to the ascent of interest in behavioral techniques, some efforts have been made to reconcile the seemingly incompatible assumptions of behavioral treatment and the more verbally oriented forms of psychotherapy (Arkowitz & Messer, 1984; Wachtel, 1977, 1984, 1994, 1997). Many of those discussions of the points of convergence bearing on psychodynamic and behavioral approaches have strongly proposed that even preliminary attempts to achieve a synthesis of these perspectives involve much more than a simple, direct translation of the terminology of one form of therapy into that of the other. However, these integrative efforts have generally been at a theoretical level, and have not really been extended in a practical way to the apparent dichotomy between these perspectives, as it emerges in the daily life and treatment experiences in today's residential treatment setting.

An important task for clinical leaders in today's residential treatment settings is to find an integrative approach to these two seeming dichotomies, which can otherwise transmit very different, even conflicting impressions to residents of the treatment center. For example, the prescriptions of the medical or technological model could well convey a message of mental disease, with a picture of the resident viewed as sick and the passive recipient of treatment from professionals who have a special power and knowledge. On the other hand, many assumptions of the milieu therapy or therapeutic community orientation, especially those promoting the acquisition of independent living skills, convey the idea that the residents should be *active* participants, be responsible for actions in their life, and be conducive to mutual communication and respect in the environment (Hoffman &

Singer, 1977). If this type of confusion of messages to residents does exist, open acknowledgement and an ongoing attempt to achieve some synthesis of the dichotomies could mitigate the potential emotional damage of mixed, double-bind messages from the two models.

CHILD AND MILIEU:
TENSIONS BETWEEN GROUP AND INDIVIDUAL CARE

Bettelheim's Thoughts on Individual Therapy Within the Milieu

Regarding the child most appropriate for residential treatment, Bettelheim at first proposed that milieu therapy was the treatment of choice both for children whose ability to maintain contact with parental figures had been catastrophically destroyed, as well as for those children who apparently had not acquired the tools for establishing such a relationship in the first place (Bettelheim & Sylvester, 1949a). Thus, according to Bettelheim, milieu therapy was most indicated where the basic needs of the child had been so neglected that the child, in Bettelheim's view, lacked psychological integration at even the pregenital level of development (according to the classical drive-theory model). For children who had achieved a higher level of integration, presenting more neurotic disturbances, psychotherapy alone might be indicated (for example, in situations where a disturbance in the Oedipal phase occasioned a regression to earlier developmental stages as a point of fixation). In such instances, Bettelheim felt, an interpersonal relationship with a psychotherapist alone could be anticipated to develop and to help in resolving the prior traumatization.

In another attempt to specify his understanding of the milieu, Bettelheim described what he understood to be the most important differences between individual psychiatric treatment and milieu care (Bettelheim, 1949). First, he pointed out that the then prevalent psychiatric techniques had been developed in treating adults, concentrating on uncovering the repressed and changing deviate personality structures. However, Bettelheim believed that for those children most in need of residential milieu treatment, emotional difficulties stemmed both from their basic inability to organize their personalities in the first place and from a near *absence* of repressive defensive mechanisms. According to Bettelheim, "the psychiatric school's therapeutic task is to bring order into chaos rather than to reorganize a deviately put together cosmos" (Bettelheim, 1949, p. 91). In other words, whereas the traditional or classical model of individual psychiatric treatment often aimed toward permitting greater instinctual gratification by lifting repression, the education of the psychiatric school was aimed more toward the socialization of wild, overpowering instinctual tendencies. Bettelheim's position regarding repression was somewhat reversed a few years later, when he began writing about infantile autism, where the amelioration of the effects of massive and dysfunctional repression became one of the *aims* of his theory of treatment for the autistic child.

Second, in Bettelheim's view, the prevalent schools of psychiatry in his time regarded the transference relationship, specifically the development of the transference neurosis, and its exploration and resolution, as the major ingredient of successful individual psychodynamic treatment, presupposing the previous existence of important relationships, feelings about which could be transferred onto the therapist. He concluded that children needing milieu treatment characteristically had experienced *no* relationships which were suitable as a vehicle for transference. This led to Bettelheim's belief that residential treatment should be largely focussed on the present, on the promotion of ego strengths in the context of daily living tasks. Therefore, according to Bettelheim, milieu therapy should be most attentive to experiences in the present, while individual psychotherapy was more appropriately concerned with events from the past. A "psychiatric residential school" needed to be much more concerned with helping the child order the world of the present, while psychiatric treatment was seen as more concerned with doing away with misinterpretations of past experiences. In Bettelheim's milieu setting, "instead of reliving the pathogenic past, the child is helped to live successfully in the present. Convincing demonstrations of ego strength thus take the place of speculation about the possible sources of its weaknesses" (Bettelheim, 1949, p. 93). Again, this was a hypothesis that Bettelheim later seemed to modify, when he wrote more specifically about the treatment of autistic children (Bettelheim, 1967).

Bettelheim gave the issue of the relationship and tension between individual psychotherapy and milieu therapy in the residential setting considerable attention, but his writings about this treatment issue tended to be somewhat contradictory and equivocable. This tension between individual and group care persists in the treatment setting of the

Orthogenic School, an as yet unresolved polarity which may be characteristic of residential treatment centers in general. Initially, Bettelheim seemed to dismiss the usefulness of individual therapy in residential care on the basis of clinical assumptions about the kinds of problems presented by children he deemed most appropriate for residential treatment. To recapitulate, Bettelheim felt that individual psychotherapy, as he understood it, was characterized by the lifting of repressions, the development of transference in the treatment relationship, and a predominant focus upon the past. These elements of individual psychotherapy seemed to make individual treatment incompatible with milieu therapy, which aimed to strengthen ego controls over unmodulated impulses and was more attentive to life in the present.

Nevertheless, despite Bettelheim's arguments that individual psychotherapy had little to offer for children in need of residential treatment, such treatment was in fact formally provided to some children at the Orthogenic School during its early years, both within the school and by therapists outside the school. For example, one of the earliest examples of the richly detailed case studies of children at the school appears to be based upon insights derived from a boy's individual psychotherapy sessions at the school, possibly with Dr. Emmy Sylvester (Bettelheim & Sylvester, 1950). In fact, the clarity and persuasiveness of that particular study's narrative style was to become a model for Bettelheim's later reconstructive case studies of delinquent, schizophrenic and autistic children. In *Love Is Not Enough* (1950), his first book about the school, Bettelheim appeared to moderate his position against psychotherapy in the milieu, noting that "'somewhere along the line of his rehabilitation . . . [the child] . . . must learn to form and manage more lasting, more intense and mature relations than those he can form within the group" (1950, p. 243).

The child *did* need, it turned out, the experience of a private, long term relationship with an adult to clear away "the residues of the more distant past." However, while the "so-called individual sessions" had many things in common with child psychotherapy, Bettelheim felt that they had functions which, in his view, exceeded those usually provided by traditional forms of psychotherapy, including the provision of a private setting for the discharge of strong aggression and negativism (rather than in the group setting), to allow regressive behaviors, and to provide educative guidance for acquiring basic social interaction skills.

The individual sessions also clearly differed from classical forms of psychotherapy in other ways, including: (1) the use of staff members who had little or no formal training in the provision of psychotherapy as "individual session" persons, and (2) the very close inter-relation between the individual treatment experience and the reality of group life (for example, a staff person might have served both as a child's group counselor and as the individual session person). However, by providing his model of private sessions, Bettelheim was attempting to resolve the seeming differences between individual and milieu therapy by the compromise of offering "individual sessions" which had some commonalities to individual child therapy, but which in many ways seemed to be quite different from formal psychotherapy.

Persisting Discrepancies Between Individual and Group Care

Despite Bettelheim's efforts to deal with this polarity of individual versus milieu therapy in the residential treatment setting, the tension between the two modes of treatment was never clearly resolved. This difficulty is revealed even today in the persistence of a number of treatment issues. At a more theoretical level, a number of factors may contribute to the tension between individual and group care in the residential setting. First, even within a cohesive psychodynamic group milieu, one might find individual therapists providing a wide range of sometimes divergent forms of psychodynamic psychotherapy, ranging from classical drive and ego one-person psychologies, to some of the more contemporary approaches. Further, especially given the time-constraints of current residential funding sources, one might speculate that more therapists today are turning to shorter-term, more reality-oriented treatment approaches, with an increase in the use of the behavioral and cognitive-behavior perspectives.

Even given the potential diversity of approaches in individual therapy, it is highly likely that the individual model of treatment is a one-person psychology model, with assumptions which are divergent from, or logically incompatible with, the intrinsically interpersonal life of the residential setting. In addition, this kind of difficulty can be further aggravated when both the individual treatment *and* the milieu setting are seen only through the lens of the one-person psychology model, in effect systematically invalidating the residents' real perceptions that their "world" in the treatment center is essentially a two-person, interpersonal experience, potentially nullifying their sense of credibility and self-worth. Again, as proposed in the previous section, promoting a two-person or even constructivist approach in the understanding of both the individual and group care experiences of the residents is essential when possible, and where this is not feasible it is crucial to strive for some integration of the one/two-person dichotomies in the general treatment setting.

In settings which pose fundamental obstacles to efforts at integration of those dichotomies, Altman (1993, 1995) has extended the two-person relational model of individual therapy to a broader, hypothetical "three-person" model, where the third person in the individual treatment process represents the context of the socioeconomic status of the patient, as well as the institutional characteristics of the treatment setting. For Altman, his three-person model further enables the therapist to recognize, for example, the external setting for individual relational treatment (in his case, an inner-city public mental health clinic) as an analytic issue, rather than simply as an interference with the more traditional model of two people working in isolation from the reality of the institutional arrangements which surround them, or (in terms of the issues presented in this paper) from the impact of a milieu based upon clinical assumptions which are divergent from the two-person model of treatment.

Complicating the theoretical issues facing the provision of individual psychotherapy within group care settings (and there are surely many more) are a number of practical difficulties. For example, in addition to the fact that a wide variety of theoretical individual therapy orientations may be provided in the same residential treatment setting, direct-care workers in the milieu often lack formal training in or a personal experience with individual psychotherapy. On the one hand, this situation can subtly dispose individual therapists to feel and/or act as though they possess a higher, special, more powerful understanding of the patient or resident, a stance which can result in direct-care staff feeling as though they are viewed as naive and expected to simply passively cooperate with the authority and special "expertise" of the individual psychotherapist. On the other hand, even if an individual therapist emphasizes to direct-care staff the ongoing *uncertainty* of the individual therapy process, the direct-care staff could still react to personal feelings about their own lack of formal training or direct experience with an unrealistically "magical" view of the process of individual psychotherapy, feelings of suspicion and fear, or a sense of barely disguised mistrust. These reactions can be directed not only to the individual therapist's work, but also displaced onto the youth's own experience of his/her involvement in the individual therapy process.

Additional tension between the individual psychotherapy and the general milieu can arise from the fact that it can be extremely difficult for the individual therapist to richly convey the details of the techniques and interactional fabric of the individual therapy experience to other staff members in the group setting. This dilemma is seen not only in the ongoing daily life of the milieu, but it is also reflected in the general body of literature on residential treatment, where over the years there has been a striking paucity of published extended case material describing the *actual conduct* of individual psychotherapy with children in the residential milieu. Another obstacle to harmony between individual and milieu therapy is created by the sometimes subtle, though often overt, belief that individual therapy is mostly involved with the child's inner life, while milieu therapy is more concerned with experiences with others and the external milieu environment. This is, of course, another reflection of the illusory one-person/two-person psychology dichotomy. The reality is that *each* treatment modality is involved with *both* inner and outer aspects of the child's experiences, which may serve to make a resolution of the tension between the two kinds of treatment even *more* difficult in practice.

Other practical issues which emerge as a reflection of this polarity between the individual and group or milieu treatment modalities in residential care include the issue of confidentiality and trust in the individual therapy relationship conducted within a larger group care setting committed to all-staff communication. There can also occur instances of the periodic blurring of boundaries between the seemingly more transference-driven individual treatment and the child's sometimes more reality-oriented experiences of the milieu group life. Another difficulty, again related to the seeming individual/group polarity, is the periodic emergence of discrepant treatment goals for a particular child (such as rapid behavioral change versus longer-term internal growth), which can be provoked by milieu direct-care workers' understandable wishes to see a child's disruptive behaviors in the group setting quickly diminish through individual therapy interventions. The foregoing dilemmas are, of course, only an illustrative sample of the many difficult complexities which can arise between the individual and group care treatment efforts in residential settings.

CONCLUSION

In a time of concern with managed care and reduced lengths of treatment for troubled children and adolescents in the United States, we are confronted ironically with an ever larger number of children who are born in circumstances of urban social disorganization and personal despair. These are children who are often unable to benefit from traditional modes of intervention and who have been portrayed in the clinical literature as the children no one wants. Confronted with this dilemma, the present discussion of group and individual aspects of residential treatment examined certain aspects of the historical development of residential care and the concept of the therapeutic milieu in the United States. The historical review then turned to a consideration of some of the more recent advances made in our understanding of theories about treatment, specifically regarding the evolution of the two-person and constructivist views of treatment.

The brief discussion of contemporary views about therapy then led to a reconsideration of many of the persisting difficulties which even today confront our efforts to provide milieu therapy within residential treatment. The paper looked at selected illustrations of some of those difficulties, which remain embedded in contemporary discussions about group care, including: (1) the sometimes conflicting assumptions of a medical model of treatment versus milieu therapy or the therapeutic community; (2) efforts to define an appropriate psychological model to adequately describe milieu therapy or the therapeutic community; and (3) the potentially inherent conflict between the assumptions of individual psychotherapy and milieu therapy, when both are provided within the context of residential group care. This discussion did not attempt to provide answers to all the stresses which can emerge in a residential setting striving to provide a range of mental health services, nor was it intended to be a criticism of the medical model or behaviorally-oriented therapies. The intent was more simply to point out that an amalgamation of treatment models can have real consequences for children in group care. A continued *awareness* of those potential consequences is essential to mitigate their potentially anti-therapeutic effects.

REFERENCES

Adam, K. S., Keller, A. E., & West, M. Attachment organization and vulnerability to loss, separation, and abuse in disturbed adolescents. In Susan Goldberg, Roy Muir, and John Kerr (Eds.), *Attachment Theory: Social, Developmental, and Clinical Perspectives*, 309-341. Hillsdale, NJ/London: The Analytic Press.

Aichhorn, A. (1925). *Wayward Youth* (Trans. E. Bryant, J. Deming, M. O'Neil Hawkins, G. Mohr, E. Mohr, H. Ross, & H. Thun). New York: The Viking Press.

Aichhorn, A. (1964). *Delinquency and Child Guidance: Selected Papers*. (Eds. O. Fleischmann, P. Kramer, and H. Ross). New York: International Universities Press (Menninger Clinic Monograph Series No. 15).

Altman, N. (1993). Psychoanalysis and the urban poor. *Psychoanalytic Dialogues, 3* (1), 29-49.

Altman, N. (1995). *The Analyst in the Inner City: Race, Class, and Culture Through a Psychoanalytic Lens*. Hillsdale, NJ/London: The Analytic Press.

Arkowitz, H., & Messer, S. B. (1984). *Psychoanalytic Therapy and Behavior Therapy: Is Integration Possible?* New York: Plenum Press, 1984.

Bettelheim, B. (1943). Mass behavior in an extreme situation. *Journal of Abnormal and Social Psychology, 38*, 417-452.

Bettelheim, B. (1947). The concentration camp as a class state. *Modern Review, 1*, 628-637.

Bettelheim, B. (1948a). Closed institutions for children. *Bulletin of the Menninger Clinic, 1*, 135-142.

Bettelheim, B. (1948b). Somatic symptoms in superego formation. *American Journal of Orthopsychiatry, 18*, 649-658.

Bettelheim, B. (1949). A psychiatric school. *Quarterly Journal of Child Behavior, 1*, 86-95.

Bettelheim, B. (1950). *Love Is Not Enough*. New York: Free Press.

Bettelheim, B. (1955). *Truants from Life*. New York: Free Press.

Bettelheim, B. (1956). Schizophrenia as a reaction to extreme situations. *American Journal of Orthopsychiatry, 26*, 507-518.

Bettelheim, B. (1960). *The Informed Heart*. New York: The Free Press.

Bettelheim, B. (1967). *The Empty Fortress*. New York: Free Press.

Bettelheim, B. (1974). *A Home for the Heart*. New York: Alfred A. Knopf.

Bettelheim, B., & Sylvester, E. (1947). Therapeutic influence of the group on the individual. *American Journal of Orthopsychiatry, 17*, 684-692.

Bettelheim, B., & Sylvester, E. (1948). A therapeutic milieu. *American Journal of Orthopsychiatry*, 18, 191-206.

Bettelheim, B., & Sylvester, E. (1949a). Milieu therapy: Indications and illustrations. *Psychoanalytic Review, 36*, 54-68.

Bettelheim, B., & Sylvester, E. (1949b). Physical symptoms in emotionally disturbed children. *The Psychoanalytic Study of the Child, 4*, 353-368. New York: International Universities Press.

Bettelheim, B., & Sylvester, E. (1950). Delinquency and morality. *The Psychoanalytic Study of the Child, 5*, 329-342. New York: International Universities Press.

Blase, K. A., Fixsen, D. L., Freeborn, K., & Jaeger, D. (1989). The behavioral model. In Robert D. Lyman, Steven Prentice-Dunn, and Steward Gabel (Eds.), *Residen-*

tial and Inpatient Treatment of Children and Adolescents, 43-59. New York: Plenum Press.

Blatt, S. J., & Blass, R. B. (1990). Attachment and separateness: A dialectic model of the products and processes of development throughout the life cycle. *The Psychoanalytic Study of the Child, 45*, 107-127. New Haven, CT: Yale University Press.

Bleiberg, E. (1987). Stages in the treatment of narcissistic children and adolescents. *Bulletin of the Menninger Clinic, 51* (3), 296-313.

Bollas, C. (1987). *The Shadow of the Object. Psychoanalysis of the Unknown Thought*. New York: Columbia University Press.

Borowitz, G. H. (1970). The therapeutic utilization of emotions and attitudes evoked in the caretakers of disturbed children. *British Journal of Medical Psychology, 43*, 129-139.

Brendtro, L. K., & Wasmund, W. (1989). The peer culture model. In Robert D. Lyman, Steven Prentice-Dunn, and Steward Gabel (Eds.), *Residential and Inpatient Treatment of Children and Adolescents*, 81-96. New York: Plenum Press.

Cohler, B. J. (1996). The man who cared too much: Nina Sutton's biography of Bruno Bettelheim. *Readings: A Journal of Reviews and Commentary in Mental Health, 11* (3), 13-17.

Cohler, B. J., & Zimmerman, D. P. (1997). Youth in residential care. From war nursery to therapeutic milieu. *The Psychoanalytic Study of the Child, 52*, 359-385. New Haven, CT: Yale University Press.

Cohler, B. J., & Zimmerman, D. P. (1996). On the need to be understood: Feelings of desperation and therapeutic response in a psychotic adolescent boy. *Association for Child Analysis Bulletin* (Spring, 1996).

Cooper, A. (1986). Toward a limited definition of psychic trauma. In A. Rothstein (Ed.) *The Reconstruction of Trauma: Its Significance in Clinical Work*. Madison, CT: International Universities Press, 41-58.

Dishion, T., French, D., & Patterson, G. (1995). The development and ecology of antisocial behavior. In D. Cicchetti and D. Cohen (Eds.) *Developmental Psychopathology. Volume 2: Risk, Disorder, and Adaptation*, 421-511. New York: Wiley-Interscience.

Ehrenberg, D. B. (1992). *The Intimate Edge. Extending the Reach of Psychoanalytic Interaction*. New York/London: Norton.

Ekstein, R. (1990). Preface to Peter Heller's *A Child Analysis with Anna Freud*, ix-xv. Madison, CT: International Universities Press.

Family Life Development Center (1993). *Therapeutic Crisis Intervention*. Ithaca, NY: Cornell University College of Human Ecology.

Freud, A. (1941-1945/1973). Monthly Reports to the Foster Parents' Plan for War Children, Inc., New York. In. A. Freud, *The Writings of Anna Freud, Volume III: 1939-1945*, 3-540. New York: International Universities Press.

Freud, A. (1954). The widening scope of indications for psychoanalysis. *Journal of the American Psychoanalytic Association, 2*, 607.

Freud, A., & Burlingham, D. (1944/1973). Infants without families: The case for and against residential nurseries. In. A. Freud, *The Writings of Anna Freud, Volume III: 1939-1945*, 543-664. New York: International Universities Press.

Fritsch, R. C., & Goodrich, W. (1990). Adolescent inpatient attachment as treatment process. *Adolescent Psychiatry, 17*, 246-263. Chicago, IL: The University of Chicago Press.

Gill, M. M. (1994). *Psychoanalysis in Transition: A Personal View*. Hillsdale, NJ: The Analytic Press.

Gossett, J., Lewis, J., & Barnhart, D. (1983) *To Find a Way: The Outcome of Hospital Treatment of Disturbed Adolescents*. New York: Brunner/Mazel.

Henry, J. (1954). The formal social structure of a psychiatric hospital. *Psychiatry, 17*, 139-151.

Henry, J. (1957a). Types of institutional structure. *Psychiatry, 20*, 47-60.

Henry, J. (1957b), The culture of interpersonal relations in a therapeutic institution for emotionally disturbed children. *The American Journal of Orthopsychiatry, 27*, 725-734.

Hoffman, I. Z. (1992). Some practical implications of a social-constructivist view of the psychoanalytic situation. *Psychoanalytic Dialogues, 2* (3), 287-304.

Hoffman, I. Z. (1994). Dialectical thinking and therapeutic action in the psychoanalytic process. *Psychoanalytic Quarterly, 63*, 187-218.

Hoffman, I. Z. (1998). *Ritual and Spontaneity in the Psychoanalytic Process: A Dialectical-Constructivist Approach*. Hillsdale, NJ/London: The Analytic Press.

Hoffman, I., & Singer, Paul R. (1977). The incompatibility of the medical model and the therapeutic community. *Social Science and Medicine, 11*, 425-431.

Jenuwine, M. (1990) *A History of the Orthogenic School of the University of Chicago*. Unpublished master's degree paper, University of Chicago.

Jenuwine, M., & Cohler, B. (1996). Treating the very troubled child: Conduct disorders, aggression, and the problem of DSM-IV. In J. Barron (Ed.) *Making Diagnosis Meaningful: New Psychological Perspectives*. Washington, DC: The American Psychological Association Press.

Levenson, E. (1983). *The Ambiguity of Change. An Inquiry into the Nature of Psychoanalytic Reality*. New York: Basic Books.

Lewin, K. (1941/1951). Regression, retrogression, and development. In D. Cartwright (Ed.) *Field Theory in Social Science*, 543-664. New York: Harper and Brothers.

Lewin, K. (1943/1951). Defining the "field at a given time." In D. Cartwright (Ed.) *Field Theory in Social Science*, 43-59. New York: Harper and Brothers.

Lewin, K. (1944/1951). Constructs in field theory. In D. Cartwright (Ed.) *Field Theory in Social Science*, 30-41. New York: Harper and Brothers.

Lewin, K. (1947/1951). Frontiers in group dynamics. In D. Cartwright (Ed.) *Field Theory in Social Science*, 87-129. New York: Harper and Brothers.

Lewis, W. W., & Lewis, B. L. (1989). The psychoeducational model: Cumberland House after 25 years. In Robert D. Lyman, Steven Prentice-Dunn, and Steward Gabel (Eds.), *Residential and Inpatient Treatment of Children and Adolescents*, 82-113. New York: Plenum Press.

McGlashan, T. H. (1984). The Chestnut Lodge follow-up study: I. Follow-up methodology and study sample. *Archives of General Psychiatry, 41*, 573-585.

Mitchell, S. A. (1988). *Relational Concepts in Psychoanalysis. An Integration*. Cambridge, MA/London: Harvard University Press.

Mitchell, S. A. (1997). *Influence and Autonomy in Psychoanalysis*. Hillsdale, NJ: The Analytic Press.

Ogden, T. H. (1986). *The Matrix of the Mind: Object Relations and the Psychoanalytic Dialogue*. Northvale, NJ/London: Aronson.

Racker, H. (1968). *Transference and Countertransference*. New York: International Universities Press.

Redl, F. (1942). Group emotion and leadership. *Psychiatry*, 2: 573-596.

Redl, F. (1943). Group psychological elements in discipline problems. *American Journal of Orthopsychiatry, 13*, 77-81.

Redl, F. (1944). Diagnostic group work. *American Journal of Orthopsychiatry, 14*, 53-68.

Redl, F. (1949). The phenomenon of contagion and "shock effect" in group therapy. In K. R. Eissler (Ed.), *Searchlights on Delinquency*, 315-328. New York: International Universities Press.

Redl, F., & Wineman, D. (1951). *Children Who Hate*. Glencoe, IL: The Free Press.

Redl, F., & Wineman, D. (1952). *Controls from Within*. Glencoe, IL: The Free Press.

Searles, H. F. (1965). *Collected Papers on Schizophrenia and Related Subjects*. New York: International Universities Press.

Small, R., Kennedy, K., & Bender, B. (1991). Critical issues for practice in residential treatment. *American Journal of Orthopsychiatry, 61* (3), 327-338.

Stolorow, R., & Atwood, G. (1992). *Contexts of Being. The Intersubjective Foundations of Psychological Life*. Hillsdale, NJ/London: The Analytic Press.

Sugarman, A. (1994). Trauma and abuse: An overview. In A. Sugarman (Ed.) *Victims of Abuse: The Emotional Impact of Child and Adult Trauma*. Madison, CT: International Universities Press, 1-24.

Swanson, A. J., & Schaefer, C. E. (1988). Helping children deal with separation and loss in residential placement. In Charles E. Schaefer and Arthur J. Swanson (Eds.), *Children in Residential Care: Critical Issues in Treatment*, 19-29. New York: Van Nostrand Reinhold.

Tansey, M. J. & Burke, W. F. (1989). *Understanding Countertransference. From Projective Identification to Empathy*. Hillsdale, NJ/London: The Analytic Press.

Trieschman, A., Whittaker, J., & Brendtro, L. (1969). *The Other 23 Hours: Childcare Work with Emotionally Disturbed Children*. Chicago: Aldine Publishing Company.

Wachtel, P. L. (1977). *Psychoanalysis and Behavior Therapy*. New York: Basic Books.

Wachtel, P. L. (1984). On theory, practice, and the nature of integration. In H. Arkowitz and S. B. Messer (Eds.), *Psychoanalytic Therapy and Behavior Therapy: Is Integration Possible?*, 31-52. New York: Plenum Press.

Wachtel, P. L. Behavior and experience: Allies, not adversaries. *Journal of Psychotherapy Integration, 4* (2), 121-131.

Wachtel, P. L. (1997). *Psychoanalysis, Behavior Therapy, and the Relational World*. Washington, DC: American Psychological Association.

Winnicott, D. W. (1960). The theory of the parent-infant relationship. *International Journal of Psychoanalysis, 41*, 585-595.

Young, J. E. (1938). The Orthogenic School. Unpublished report, University of Chicago, Chicago, Illinois.

Zimmerman, D. P. (1990). Notes on the history of adolescent inpatient and residential treatment. *Adolescence, 25* (97), 9-38.

Zimmerman, D. P. (1993). The little turtle's progress: A reconsideration of the short versus long-term residential treatment controversy. *Children and Youth Services Review, 15* (3), 219-243.

Zimmerman, D. P. (1994). A pilot demographic study of population changes in a residential treatment center. *Residential Treatment for Children & Youth, 11* (3), 17-33.

Zimmerman, D. P. (1997a). A biographical search for Bettelheim, the enigmatic healer: A review essay. *Residential Treatment for Children & Youth, 15* (2), 17-28.

Zimmerman, D. P. (1997b). *Bettelheim: A Life and Legacy:* On succumbing to the temptations of "celebrity biography." *Psychoanalytic Psychology, 14* (2), 279-293.

Psychotherapy in Residential Treatment: The Human Toll of Scientism and Managed Care

D. Patrick Zimmerman, PsyD

SUMMARY. This paper briefly reviews the intentions of some of the early founders of residential treatment centers for children, and then presents a discussion of contemporary efforts to comply with the insistence upon proof of treatment efficacy for group care and individual psychotherapy. The demands for empirical evaluation are considered in terms of the body of scientistic attacks upon the conceptual foundations of psychoanalysis and verbal psychotherapy, and in light of the historical emergence of managed care as a delimiting power in mental health care. The discussion concludes with a reconsideration of those attacks in light of contemporary refinements of psychoanalytic theory and technique, and then examines the implications of the objectivist perspective with regard to our broader conceptions of the treatment process, the human mind, and ideas about modern culture. *[Article copies available for a fee from The Haworth Document Delivery Service: 1-800-342-9678. E-mail address: <getinfo@haworthpressinc.com> Website: <http://www.HaworthPress. com>]*

KEYWORDS. Psychotherapy, residential treatment, managed care

A version of this paper was presented at the 42nd Annual Meeting of the American Association of Children's Residential Centers at Sanibel Island, Florida, October 16, 1998.

[Haworth co-indexing entry note]: "Psychotherapy in Residential Treatment: The Human Toll of Scientism and Managed Care." Zimmerman, D. Patrick. Co-published simultaneously in *Residential Treatment for Children & Youth* (The Haworth Press, Inc.) Vol. 18, No. 2, 2000, pp. 55-85; and: *The Forsaken Child: Essays on Group Care and Individual Therapy* (D. Patrick Zimmerman) The Haworth Press, Inc., 2000, pp. 55-85. Single or multiple copies of this article are available for a fee from The Haworth Document Delivery Service [1-800-342-9678, 9:00 a.m. - 5:00 p.m. (EST). E-mail address: getinfo@haworthpress inc.com].

INTRODUCTION: ON SCIENTISM

The ascendance of philosophical forms of objectivism and logical positivism during the past century has been associated with the emergence of a resolutely empirical and physical scientific posture, contributing to a powerful world view which has often made immodest claims about what is verifiable truth, and what is not. The agendas of objectivism and logical positivism appear to have become a matter of public impact in the fields of psychology and psychotherapy somewhat later than in some other areas of the human sciences (and this appears to be similarly the case with regard to the assimilation into psychology of more refined ideas about science, where philosophers of science themselves engaged in a revolt against positivism in the 1950s). For example, while the scientistic critique of psychoanalysis and other forms of verbal psychotherapy did not appear to gain critical impetus until the 1980s, the reductionist influences of logical positivism and the succeeding epistemological doctrine of radical historicism were matters of substantial opposition in the field of political theory in the United States as early as the 1940s (Voegelin, 1948, 1952; Strauss, 1953).

Almost fifty years ago, Voegelin (1952) described the evolution of the positivistic era in the second half of the nineteenth century in terms of the emergence of two fundamental assumptions: (1) the belief that the methods used in the mathematical sciences were possessed of some inherent virtue and that all other sciences could achieve comparable progress if they accepted mathematical methods as their model; and (2) the broader assumption that the methods of the natural sciences were a criterion for theoretical relevance in general. He further noted that from the combination of these two assumptions, there emerged the now well-known series of objectivist claims that any study of "reality" "could qualify as scientific only if it used the methods of the natural sciences, that problems couched in other terms were illusionary problems, that in particular metaphysical questions which do not admit of answers by the methods of the sciences of phenomena should not be asked, that realms of being which are not assessable to exploration by the model methods were irrelevant, and, in the extreme, that such realms of being did not exist" (1952, p. 4).

In psychology, one reaction to this state of affairs was to declare the subject of mental events, mental experience, and consciousness off limits. Later efforts to rectify this move involved the development of cognitive-behavioral psychological models and treatment techniques, which have proven to be effective in the remediation of *specific* behavioral disorders. Questions remain, however, about longer-term outcome issues, as well as the ability of such delimited techniques to help individuals suffering with more complicated personality disorders, or with behavioral problems stemming from either traumatic events or deep psychological structural issues. According to the objectivist view, psychological "science" should confine itself to behavior that is observable in ways defined by the forms of scientific inquiry concerned with non-intentional objects. In line with the procedures of this approach, the more rigid scientific perspective would preclude serious consideration of many of the psychological traits we all think and talk about as a matter of everyday life, including our beliefs, thoughts, consciousness, desires, and emotions. Humanistic issues such as these are simply left hanging by the objectivist approach, which provides an illusory solution to this dilemma by resorting to an ever more minute examination of external behavior, while ignoring the world of human intentionality. Rather than attempting to come to some new understanding of those existential issues, it denies their validity as objects for proper scientific inquiry.

The following commentary briefly reviews the intentions of the early founders of residential treatment centers for children, and then presents a discussion of contemporary efforts to comply with the insistence upon proof of treatment efficacy for group care and individual psychotherapy. The demands for empirical evaluation are considered in terms of the body of scientistic attacks upon the conceptual foundations of psychoanalysis and verbal psychotherapy, and in light of the historical emergence of managed care as a delimiting power in mental health care. The discussion concludes with a reconsideration of those attacks in light of contemporary refinements of psychoanalytic theory and technique, and then examines the implications of the objectivist perspective with regard to our broader conceptions of the treatment process, the human mind, and ideas about modern culture.

FROM COMPASSIONATE HUMANISM TO OBJECTIVIST VALIDATION

There have been many threads in the historical evolution of the concept of group care in the United States, but one of the clearest and most direct lines of theory development leads back to August Aichhorn's organization of an institution for delinquents in Austria, in 1917 (Zimmerman & Cohler, 1998). The focus of contemporary writings upon the empirical validation of program effectiveness contrasts starkly with the concerns of Aichhorn and the other early pioneers who contributed to this particular path of theory development, where understanding the realm of the inner life of troubled children was the primary concern. The passionate interests of those pioneers were basically qualitative ones, arising from wishes to deal with a variety of humanistic issues. Those issues, which provided an impetus for the greater part of that body of clinical material, included: (1) a wish to understand the character formation of anti-social young people, and to construct a benign environment for their rehabilitation (Aichhorn, 1925/1965); (2) the need to develop an understanding of early childhood developmental processes based upon observation, and to cast those processes within a general psychodynamic theory (Cohler & Zimmerman, 1997; Freud, 1941-45/1973); (3) an attempt to provide a living environment for child victims of wartime trauma, and to understand the effects of ongoing environmental violence, separation from and permanent loss of family members upon their psychological functioning (Cohler & Zimmerman, 1997; Freud, 1941-45/1973; (4) the refinement of our understanding of and management techniques for impulsive, aggressive children (Bettelheim, 1955; Bettelheim and Sylvester, 1949a,b, 1950; Redl & Wineman, 1951, 1952); and (5) a wish to expand our clinical knowledge to include a range of what had previously been considered a range of untreatable disorders, including psychosis and autism (Bettelheim, 1955, 1967; Zimmerman, 1990).

In recent years, however, there has been a noticeable shift in the literature about residential treatment in the United States away from the existential concerns which impassioned the earlier writers about group care for children. Those concerns often have been replaced by an intensified drive to scientifically prove the positive effect of residential care. There are, of course, a number of forces behind this current stress upon empirical research, including the fact that present American public policy opinion is very clearly unsupportive of residential treatment. A second determinant of the intense focus upon outcome research is related to the powerful emergence of managed care concepts within the American health system, in combination with stricter guidelines and limitations of residential and other forms of mental health care funding sources. Underlying each of these factors has been the ascent of the more widespread objectivist view in the field of mental health, associated with its demand that ultimately any worthwhile treatment program must be measurable according to the methods of natural science. Each of these issues will receive closer attention in succeeding discussions provided in the course of this paper.

Overviews of outcome evaluation in the United States strongly suggest that the attempts to comply with the demands for empirical proof of both residential treatment and individual therapy for children have yielded only a modicum of success. There appears to be agreement now that *in general* both residential treatment (Curry, 1986, 1991, 1995; Pfeiffer, 1989; Pfeiffer, & Strzelecki, 1990) and individual child psychotherapy (Barrnett, Docherty, & Frommelt, 1991; Casey & Berman, 1985; Smith, Glass, & Miller, 1980; Tramontana, 1980; Wright, Moelis, & Pollack, 1976) have beneficial effects. In England, researchers' work with the Hampstead Index have reached similar positive conclusions about the beneficial effect of long-term individual treatment for children (Bolland & Sandler, 1961; Fonagy & Target, 1996, 1997; Sandler, Kennedy, & Tyson, 1980). For both residential care and individual child psychotherapy, however, serious obstacles remain with regard to effectively demonstrating exactly *what* works when studying a particular form of treatment, or when comparing different forms of treatment.

Bachrach, Galatzer-Levy, Skolnikoff, and Waldron (1991) reached similar conclusions about the question of long-term (analytic) treatment outcome with adults. Despite the observations of those reviewers that a number of empirical studies have generally confirmed that patients suitable for that model of long-term treatment actually do derive benefit, they concluded that: " . . . quantitative studies, in particular, have not contributed fresh insights into psychoanalysis, nor have they demonstrated findings with substantially greater rigor than previous clinical investigations. They have not added in a significant way to our clinical fund of knowledge, nor have they clarified formulations which have long been a part of psychoanalytic lore" (Bachrach et al., 1991, p. 910). In other words, the naturalistic empirical approach appears to function better with the kind of data involved in determining the quality of treatment outcome than when it is applied to issues involving the actual treatment process.

The objectivist, empirical response to this dilemma is to consider that these obstacles merely present further methodological problems yet to be resolved. Others, who are more persuaded of the humanistic dimensions of treatment, suggest that the obstacles to proving *what* works reflect the fact that there are some things which are not measurable by the observational methods of natural science. Paradoxically, then, the degree of progress that we have made in evaluating treatment failure or success leads us back to a reconsideration of the extent to which the validation of residential and individual treatment can rightly be made subservient to the rules of material science, and to what extent might they be more appropriately understood differently.

SCIENCE AS IDEOLOGY: THE EVASION OF UNCERTAINTY

The successful emergence of managed care as a corporate power in the United States has been related to its ability to constrict the range of services that it will sanction, often supported by the demand for objectivist treatment validation for approved health-care services. Eist (1997) has provided a concise, but striking overview of the cultural forces which provided impetus to the shift from what some view as the somewhat more socially-responsive American form of health insurance initially founded in the 1930s to protect citizens suffering from serious illnesses from imminent financial ruin, to the more financially pre-occupied, profit-motivated industry which exists today. Two critical components of this industry have been established to maximize cost containment: (1) managed care review corporations established to provide utilization control of patient services for private insurance companies; and (2) specialized group health insurance plans or Health Maintenance Organizations (HMOs), which offer their enrollees medical services which are circumscribed and often available only from professionals who are members of the particular provider HMO network. Critics of today's managed-care industry in the United States (Eist, 1997) argue that it justifies its existence by claiming to reduce cost and improve quality, while providing significant rewards to those who accomplish this task. However, some claim that it has too often failed on the first two of these counts, neither reducing costs nor improving quality.

In terms of mental health care, standard HMO group coverage in the United States usually provides only brief forms of therapy for conditions deemed responsive to brief intervention. It often denies more in-depth or longer-term private care services to others with more serious disorders, shifting them to services provided by the already overly-burdened public sector. The practices of managed care companies have also seriously eroded mental health training and research programs, and have sometimes cut mental health patient benefits by as much as 80 percent (Eist, 1997). Too often, the savings that are realized by managed care are achieved by increasingly denying the elderly, poor, minority, young, and disabled citizens access to the very health care services they often desperately require.

The arguments used in the managed-care restriction of many forms of mental health services, associated with the demands for objective validation of treatment effectiveness, receive support from the kind of thinking typical of the scientistic critiques of psychodynamic forms of treatment (including psychoanalytic and other forms of verbal psychotherapy), which have escalated during the past two decades in the United States. In America, the ascension of the doubts about and arguments against the "scientific" status of psychoanalysis reached its peak in the 1980s with the publication of a number of sharply critical commentaries by Adolph Grunbaum, a philosopher of science (1982, 1984, 1988, 1993). His skeptical conclusions about psychoanalysis have served as a model for the arguments against the usefulness of psychoanalysis, and have been extended by others to apply as well to psychodynamic and other forms of verbal psychotherapy.

While there have been extensive rebuttals of Grunbaum's positivist attacks (for example, since 1984 more than 80 major articles responding to his critique have appeared in the indexed psychological literature), for much of the general public, it has been largely the attacks, the Freud-doubting and bashing, which have filtered down from this heated debate. The resulting present-day climate of doubt in the general public about psychotherapy in the United States has been extended to include frequent questions about the worth of longer-term group care models of residential treatment for young people. Small, Kennedy, and Bender (1991) have noted that current American public policy opinion has become very clearly unsupportive of residential treatment. At best, the public policy message today is that residential treatment should be used only as an intervention of last resort, that length of stay should be limited, and that the main planning goal should be the permanent reunification of children with their families.

While it is beyond the scope of the present discussion to present a detailed discussion of Grunbaum's critique, it is important to summarize selected major points in his arguments. First, it is important to note that historically the critiques of classical models of psychoanalysis came from at least two different vantage points and that they proceeded with divergent purposes: (1) one body of questions which came from within the field of psychoanalysis itself and aimed for a reformulation of the more objectively-toned classical beliefs about knowledge and authority in the treatment setting; and (2) a second group of dismissive arguments was advanced by critics from other professional fields, which often relied upon a more rigid scientistic rejection of classical beliefs as their paradigm and generalized those arguments to other forms of verbal treatment. The reassessments of classical ideas from within psychoanalysis led to contemporary reformulations of analytic theory and technique which have included contemporary, two-person models of theory and technique, such as the intersubjective, relational, and social-constructive perspectives. The second type of critique, the positivist arguments made from external vantage points, have tended to promote a rigid, over-generalized repudiation of the very possibility of establishing validity for psychotherapy treatment. These arguments made no effort to strive for any useful redefinitions of treatment, which would in turn reflect the advancements made in scientific thinking, beyond the outmoded positivist model (which has long since been repudiated by more refined scientific thinking).

It is the positivist thinking advanced by the second type of argument, the radically dismissive positions from external critics, which strengthens the destructive limits placed upon longer-term psychotherapy and group care. As a primary advocate for this perspective, Grunbaum insisted that psychoanalysis and psychotherapy needed to be bound by the same rules of validation demanded by the natural sciences. According to Grunbaum, this demand was justified for two reasons: (1) Freud himself had claimed that psychoanalysis was part of the natural sciences, and (2) since Freud talked about many of his hypotheses as *causal*, they therefore had to be testable and falsifiable by the usual methods of natural science. With regard to that second claim, Grunbaum asserted that psychoanalytic theory inevitably fails by the standards of natural science, primarily because data from the psychoanalytic process is irretrievably contaminated by therapist suggestion and direction.

Transitions in Psychoanalytic Theory and Technique

Grunbaum's scientistic arguments were originally directed specifically against the foundations of Freudian or classical forms of psychoanalysis. However, as previously noted, over the years this kind of objectivist argument has been extended by often unexamined inference to the more general fields of individual psychotherapy and residential care, permeating the climate of professional and public opinion about both of these forms of mental health care. Therefore, while *some* of the following discussion *appears* to focus more specifically upon psychoanalysis, it really does also apply more generally to the current depreciation of the fields of psychotherapy and group care, and to the crises we all face in attempting to provide those services today to children in distress. Further, the repudiation of psychotherapy has inevitable meaning for the field of residential treatment, implications which extend far beyond the simple fact that arguments against one mode of treatment have been displaced to another.

In a very real sense there are a number of historically-influenced theoretical and practical associations between these two modes of care. First of all, influences upon theories of individual psychotherapy interpenetrate with conceptual models of group care, since most models of residential care were originally derived from particular theories of individual treatment. Second, changes in conceptualizations about individual treatment, as well as in the views of models of child development often associated with particular theories of treatment, can in turn have implications for the kind of caregiver/child interventions promoted in the milieu setting. Third, individual psychotherapy is usually provided as an integral part of the broader number of services provided by residential treatment in the United States and, even though it is only part of the wider range of therapeutic activities, it often comes to serve as the paradigm or standard for the therapeutic tone of the milieu in general. Finally, although the early forms of group care were originally seen as ancillary and perhaps subordinate to the traditional, more rigidly defined models of psychodynamic psychotherapy, new directions in the understanding of psychodynamic treatment have come to reflect assumptions long promoted in the activities of milieu treatment.

Returning to Grunbaum's contentions, he claimed that his scientifically logical analysis repudiated the foundations of psychoanalysis in general (and, by implication, many other models of individual and group care), even though his arguments focussed mainly upon the assumptions and claims of the classical Freudian model. The scientific posture of his arguments was bolstered by a reliance upon techniques and findings extrapolated from the field of physics, but his positions were sometimes flawed by basic misunderstandings about either the methods or the conclusions of physics. For example, examining Grunbaum's descriptions of electrodynamic systems and the hysteresis effect in light of his actual understanding of physics, Berger (1995) demonstrated that Grunbaum argued from *partial* truths about the details of those two examples, and that he actually presented an artificial, circumscribed reading of the laws of physics in order to create the *illusion* that historicity and context are essential features not only of human life, but also of physical systems in the natural world.

Second, despite Grunbaum's claim to repudiate the foundations of psychoanalysis in general, and by implication many other models of individual and group care, his arguments really only applied to the objectivist claims and assumptions about knowledge and therapist authority, the classical Freudian model. However, the dramatic evolution of psychodynamic conceptions in theory and technique in recent years has taken the field far from many of the Freudian "foundations" that Grunbaum attacked (Altman, 1993, 1995; Bollas, 1987; Ehrenberg, 1992; Gill, 1994; Hoffman, 1994; Levenson, 1983; Mitchell, 1988, 1997; Ogden, 1986; Racker, 1968; Searles, 1965; Stolorow & Atwood, 1992; Tansey & Burke, 1989). For example, many of the scientistic arguments are directed against the Freudian claims for *retrospective insight* as the major helpful factor in classical treatment, portraying the inevitable intrusions of therapist suggestion as contaminants to the very possibility of a patient ever really achieving such true insight. Contemporary thinking, on the other hand, emphasizes the potential richness of the patient-therapist *relationship* as a major mutative factor, rather than the achievement of insights about the past alone. With this relationship seen as a forum for exploring *new* forms of experience (as well as for coming to new ways of understanding past experiences), relational psychotherapy and milieu treatment have become much more than the classically understood backward-looking stage upon which the repetition of old, childhood dramas are simply played out and finally understood.

In line with those changes, there have been substantial revisions in our understanding of the role of the therapist, which in turn have serious effects upon a major thread of the scientistic critique. For example, there has been a movement away from viewing the therapist's personally expressive activities as simply malignant, unavoidable intrusions into the treatment process, toward an appreciation of the therapist's active participation as part of an ongoing current with a valuable purpose (Racker, 1968; Gill, 1994; Hoffman, 1992a, 1994, 1998; Mitchell, 1997). Further, there is a more open awareness and acceptance of therapists' influences in terms of support, suggestion, and direction, along with a more positive assessment of those actions. Finally, rather than limiting the therapist's stance to one of medically antiseptic abstinence and interpretation, the relational perspective views therapeutic relational *experience* and the creation of meaning in that relationship as important mutative factors, as part of a mixture which includes the achievement of insights about the past. This shift reflects more than simply a change in focus; it recognizes that the issue is not simply arriving at understandings about the past, but also emphasizes the need to find ways to generate new forms of action from those insights.

Therefore, contemporary perspectives have for some time rejected the classical illusion of therapist neutrality and the chimerical attempts to avoid the appearance of suggestion and influence, circumventing the scientistic view of suggestion as malignant. While the radical empiricist demands from psychoanalysis an argument against the claim that suggestion contaminates psychoanalytic data, he fails to see that a large dimension of the development of psychoanalysis beyond Freud has been the development of techniques *to deal with* the ubiquity of suggestion. Psychoanalysis may thus be seen as distinctive *precisely* in this direct engagement with suggestion as ubiquitous, and the more dogmatic forms of scientism as distinctive in their inveterate search for a version of truth that is rid of it (Jacobson, 1996). In other words, the issue that requires continued examination is not the scientistic one of whether suggestion exists, but rather how it is handled and how it influences our clinical work (Schwartz, 1996, p. 509).

Finally, a fairly large group of contemporary clinical thinkers is allied with versions of what is called the hermeneutic tradition, where the issue of meanings created in the clinical interactions are considered to have significant importance, in addition to the issue of empirical validation (Cooper, 1993; Galatzer-Levy & Cohler, 1990; Geha, 1993; Habermas, 1971; Ricoeur, 1974; Spence, 1982, 1983; Spezanno, 1993). This perspective need not deny the importance of the issue of empirical validation, nor the conviction that real experience does matter and sometimes in fact can be validated. However, the meaning-oriented treatment process is said to fall *outside* the realm of the more rigid forms of natural science demands. As described earlier, this focus upon wishes and meaning, rather than causal "truths," views personal human meaning as context-dependent, therefore depending upon a history of experience which is not considered to be present in the more rigid theories of natural science. For example, unlike the natural objects of legitimate scientific investigation, humans self-reflectively create *meaning* about their pasts; it is often a matter of uncertainty *how* past experiences or history count for present behavior, not simply *that* it counts.

BENEATH THE SCIENTISTIC ATTACKS

As argued earlier, the rise and sometimes unquestioned acceptance of scientistic or objectivist ways of thinking is responsible for the credibility of the radical critique of verbal psychotherapy, which often has been used to provide justification for managed care guidelines in the field of mental health. It has provided managed care with considerable rhetorical weight in the name of "science" to make decisions to approve certain kinds of treatment which more closely seem to approximate science, while making strident efforts to exclude forms of treatment which do not fit the objectivist definition of science. Grunbaum's attack upon psychoanalysis stands as a model for this radical critique, and the very mention of his arguments today gives a cloak of scientific legitimacy to any commentary attempting to dismiss the legitimacy of verbal psychotherapy as a useful form of treatment. The preceding discussion addressed certain particular aspects of the scientistic thesis. However, it is also instructive to look beneath the unrelenting stream of attacks upon Freud and psychoanalysis, to comment upon the *culture of criticism* (Lear, 1998) which continues to support the attacks.

In some ways, the field of psychoanalysis in America set itself up for the intense scrutiny it has received in recent years (Galatzer-Levy, 1995; Lear, 1998; Mitchell, 1997, pp. 207-208). First, American psychoanalysis emerged as an exclusionary guild in the 1920s, restricting training and practice to medical doctors in order to take full advantage of the idealization of the medical profession with which the American public has viewed physicians throughout much of this century. Through the years, the political management of psychoanalysis was almost Stalinist in tone, and "the reigning political powers within psychoanalysis . . . hardly allowed psychoanalytic theorizing to flourish in an atmosphere of freedom and open exchange" (Mitchell, 1997, p. 208). As Lear (1998) notes, the inflated claims that psychoanalysis made for itself during the 1950s and 1960s, along with its uncritical idealization of Freud, served ultimately to make psychoanalysis a victim of self-inflicted wounds. Its own wishful self-image resulted in clinical promises it simply could not keep.

However, that being said, it is instructive to take a closer look at the currents of the scientistic criticism of psychoanalysis as the paradigm of verbal therapy. First, the criticism of Freud's thinking often involves a rejection of one of the central constructs of psychoanalysis, namely, the theory that unconscious processes can play a powerful role in the formation of a person's everyday experience. Second, the portrayal of suggestion in verbal psychotherapy as an inevitable contaminant serves to obscure the fact that even very early writings about psychoanalytic technique made stringent attempts to safeguard against therapist influence. In that sense, it stands as the first form of therapy to envision *freedom* as a primary goal, rather than some particular, circumscribed definition of human *contentment* (Lear, 1998, p. 22). Where psychoanalysis leaves it largely to patients to determine general goals for themselves, other forms of therapy *prescribe particular* outcomes, such as relieving depression, manipulating a specific behavioral change, or increasing self-esteem. The shift in modern psychoanalysis to a position which acknowledges analyst suggestion and influence continues to preserve the commitment to patient freedom as a primary goal, by openly declaring that analyst participation and enactments provide important material for mutual examination in the analytic process, and that there is in fact no value for the analyst to attempt to hide behind the guise of analyst neutrality.

Further, the demand that causal relevance for the explanatory methods of psychoanalytic practice must be established in the same manner as empirical science fails to acknowledge that the convictions achieved by clinicians and their patients in the treatment process "rest upon an intuitive, pragmatic credibility, a kind of enriched common sense" (Mitchell, 1997, p. 209). Nagel (1995) has described psychoanalytic knowledge viewed from this perspective as an extension of "common sense psychology," comprised of the basic ways that we try to make sense of our interactions with other people. To deny the usefulness of psychoanalytic explanation because it does not offer causal explanations in the same manner as empirical science is in fact to cast aside our ordinary ways of making interpretations about our everyday experiences, since those are hardly any more amenable to scientific proof. It seems that every kind of interpretive activity based upon beliefs, desires, and historical context would become open to skeptical scientistic challenge. However, no rational person would suggest that we abandon the fields of history, political science, sociology, or economics for the same scientistic reasons that Grunbaum and others would discard psychoanalysis.

Mitchell (1997, pp. 209-210) has proposed that whether the knowledge provided by these areas of the social sciences, as well as by psychoanalysis, are best categorized as science, social science, or hermeneutics is much less important than the recognition and appreciation of these kinds of knowledge and their legitimacy as credible, plausible explanations of functioning in a world of other people. Beyond the philosophical tautologies of radical empiricists, it is simply true that in endeavors to make meaningful interpretations about human things which are more ambiguous than factual, one has to employ different methods of validation than in physics or chemistry, and that this difference does not mean that they are deficient in comparison to the natural science methods (Feynman, 1998). As Lear (1998) observes:

> If psychoanalysis were to imitate the methods of physical science, it would be useless for interpreting people. Psychoanalysis is an extension of our ordinary psychological ways of interpreting people in terms of their beliefs, desires, hopes, and fears. . . . In fact, it is a sign of the success of psychoanalysis as an interpretive science that its causal claims cannot be validated in the same way as those in the physical sciences. (p. 25)

Only by resisting the temptation to give passive assent to the arguments against psychoanalysis, and likewise by refusing to limit our responses to the scientistic logic of those critiques, are we really able to begin to grasp the nature of the real objects of those attacks, which would otherwise remain obscured. Fourcher (1996) sees the *real* challenge of Grunbaum's arguments against psychoanalysis as an attempt to confirm the power of the most conservative form of intellectualism in the name of scientific authority (p. 516). According to Fourcher, Grunbaum uses rhetorical maneuvers in the guise of philosophical logic to defend the rules of science, but this defense serves mainly to establish the hegemony of a certain definition of rationality, a definition which also implies certain convictions about the relationship between thought and action. For Grunbaum, this idea of rationality, the primacy of "pure reason," demands that theory rules action, or it simply isn't true. Human purposive activity is acknowledged only to the extent that it is motivated by conscious, conceptual thought, subservient to the rules of logic. In the resulting imposed dichotomy between knowledge and action, as well as between the knower and the known, rational thought is argued to be the unquestioned controlling authority over the realm of experience and action.

One implication of this position for psychotherapy is the reification of treatment "rituals" and techniques: "Knowledge is . . . related to action only unilaterally through the objectification of the therapist's activity as 'technique,' or through the objectification of the patient's actions as expressions of some conceptual logic or rule articulated by the theory" (Fourcher, p. 524). The Grunbaum debate, then, ultimately attempts to reestablish a regime of authoritarian "rationality," where pure intellectualism strives to dominate and control the world of action and experience. Intellectualism in the form of pure reason is the antithesis of social action and engagement, and to that extent is *asocial*. Yet, as Fourcher notes, the context of our actions in general, and in particular within the actual psychotherapy treatment process, must always be defined in *social* terms (Fourcher, p. 517).

Fourcher saw the assertion of the power of intellectualism as the real challenge beneath the manifest level of the scientistic argument, and Lear (1998) described his understanding of the consequences of that challenge as an attack upon our culture's *very view of human existence*. As Lear (1998) has cogently observed, "The real object of attack–for which Freud is only a stalking horse–is the very idea that humans have unconscious motivation. A battle may be fought over Freud, but the war is over our culture's image of the human soul. Are we to see humans as having depth–as complex psychological organisms who generate layers of meaning which lie beneath the surface of their own understanding? Or are we to take ourselves as transparent . . . to treat human existence as straightforward?" (p. 27).

But the real issue is probably not simply a battle over what is unconscious and therefore scientifically unknowable, versus a conscious world which is transparently knowable. While the scientistic challenge does advance the insistence that there is no face value to the realm of the unconscious, it also impacts our view of *conscious* experience. In other words, whereas Lear sees the main thrust of scientistic thinking as an attack upon the realm of unconscious motivation, this is only one aspect of the scientistic challenge. In fact, the problem is not simply that the unconscious is ambiguous and therefore not amenable to scientific truth; humans inhabit a world of *conscious* experience which is *similarly* ambiguous. Scientistic thinking would have us believe that we can achieve truth about our conscious selves and experiences, where in reality there are some human things which are indeed factual, but many other important human things which are more ambiguous and indeterminate.

The emergence of today's profusion of rapid-repair home remedies geared to temporary narcissistic rejuvenation may be seen as a response to the refusal to recognize the mysterious and sometimes tragic dimensions of life, which are in turn anchored in the ambiguities of *both* unconscious and conscious dimensions of human experience. It is this broader rejection of ambiguity and uncertainty in our everyday lives which fosters the illusory hopes offered by the present-day explosion of self-help books about diet programs, exercise plans, techniques for finding the right romantic partner, practical schemes promising the quick accumulation of financial wealth, and various homespun remedies for the alleviation of specific neurotic symptoms. Each of these practical strategic programs promises shortcuts to a particular version of human happiness, claiming to have exclusive knowledge about what the elusive nature of that happiness really is. According to Lear, the tunnel-visioned conviction that there are such shortcuts to human perfection signals a culture which is all too eager to ignore the deep, complex, and often darker dimensions of human existence. But the driven cultural repudiation of Freud, and by implication of psychoanalysis and most forms of verbal psychotherapy, is not just a repudiation of the deep and unconscious dimensions of human experience, but it really involves the more broad-ranging attempt to avoid the more troubling questions about *both* unconscious and conscious human motivation and what makes life meaningful for an individual.

There are, of course, specific *political* implications of the scientistically-based cultural view that ignores the ambiguity of much of human motivation. The short-sighted approach to meaning as valid only to the extent that it is revealed by the straightforward application of reason results in a particular opinion about what citizens are like in our democratic society. This view depicts humans largely as preference-expressing political atoms measured by political polls, or as consumer units reflected by the fluctuations of daily stock-exchange reports. In both cases, society becomes an aggregate of these atoms, and the only irrationality recognized in their existence is the failure of these preference-expressing units to conform to the rules of behavioral, learning, or rational-choice theories (Lear, 1998, p. 29). In contradistinction, the claim of psychoanalysis is that the world is *not* entirely rational, and the techniques of psychoanalysis are partly an attempt to take the ambiguities of both unconscious and conscious motivations into account in ways that makes them less likely to disrupt human life in confusing and sometimes destructive ways.

The attack upon Freud then becomes less an assault upon the father of psychoanalysis as upon the idea of indeterminacy in life, an attack upon the belief that we are free agents in determining the courses of our lives, but also that as free agents there is no final resolution of indeterminacy through ever-more careful attention to ourselves in the efforts to determine our "true" aims and to decide which compromises in life are ultimately "best" (Hoffman, 1998). In Hoffman's view, with the acceptance of this kind of indeterminacy, there is an awareness that ambiguity is not temporary, but rather that ultimately ambiguity is irreducible. Human choice always involves choosing one course of action, while abandoning others, some of which may be in some respects equally preferable. The attempt to restrict the foundation of human choices to empirical rules obscures the ambiguity inherent in many of our important decisions by creating the myth that there are some good ways and some bad ways, and that ultimately we can always come to "know" the differences between those paths. But in many important decisions to do something, there is no linear, temporal relationship between thought and action. In those cases, our choices emerge largely as an expression of an indefinite number of both formulated and unformulated influences within the individual's experiences (Stern, 1997; Hoffman, 1992a, Hoffman, 1998).

The scientific assault represents an evasion of the belief that humans are in the painful condition of having the potential to make more meanings than we can knowingly grasp, an evasion through the flight into the illusion of scientific certainty and the wish that human choices could ultimately be technologically rational (Lear, 1998, p. 32; Hoffman, 1998). But in fact, since there are many things which *cannot* be found out by the methods of natural science and practical reason, the conviction spreads within our culture that we *do not need* to find out about these things. And then, since we do not need to find out about certain things, in a sense we come to live in the fantasy that somehow we *already know* about all of the things that *really* matter. Lear has described this illusory equation of science with certainty as leading to a culture of "knowingness" (Lear, 1998, p. 34).

With the glorification of the rational mind, pure reason becomes associated with the belief that only it can solve any problem, an association which is made possible by the fact that it cannot or refuses to acknowledge the kinds of existential problems it cannot methodically solve. The claim to "already know" distorts any real attempts to discover or find out about dimensions of meaning and life which do not conform to the belief that practical reason can solve every problem. And this, according to Lear, is the true essence of the attacks upon Freud and psychoanalysis, the advancement of a dangerous belief that if psychoanalytic ways of thinking can be empirically discounted, there will no longer be any need to either recognize or account for the fact that ultimately the world of human motivation and meaning is ambiguous. In other words, killing Freud ultimately stands for a reaffirmation of the scientific self-assurance that all real human problems can be both formulated and resolved solely through the readily apparent, methodical application of practical, scientistic reason. Unfortunately, it also stands to some degree as a renunciation of the uniquely human freedom we each exercise in ultimately being responsible for choosing our own particular courses of action in life (Hoffman, 1998).

THERAPEUTIC INTERACTION AND HUMAN AGENCY: THE JOURNEY IS THE GOAL

This paper began with a discussion of the deep concerns which led to the early efforts to develop therapeutic models of group care for children. In contrast to the early optimism about the promise of individual and group care for children, the present-day climate of opinion about mental health services is driven by a sense of crisis reflected in a loss of public confidence in the promises of group care and individual psychotherapy, especially psychoanalytically-oriented models, seen in conjunction with the ascendance of corporate managed care which not only limits, but also strives to *define* the provision of mental health treatment. The controlling influence of scientistic thinking has served as the foundation for the attacks upon psychoanalysis and verbal psychotherapy, and it has come to serve as the bedrock for the legitimacy claimed by managed care for its treatment mandates. Grunbaum's critique of psychoanalysis has served as a model for present-day efforts to assault psychodynamic ways of thinking about treatment, even though the demand that psychoanalysis present the same level and kind of proof as the natural sciences often rests upon mendacious forms of logic.

The growth and aggregation of the power of scientistic thinking in the mental health field has had grave consequences. First, there has been the rush to comply with the empirical demands of the scientistic managed care climate, floridly illustrated by our intense preoccupations with producing acceptable efficacy and effectiveness studies. However, the results of this flurry of outcome research activity has provided equivocal results. On the one hand, there has been has general validation for what we have already believed to be true, that individual and group therapeutic care *does* have a positive effect. On a perhaps more important level, however, the strategies of empirical research have generally failed in the attempt to isolate the particular ingredients within the treatment process which account for those changes. The empiricists explain this inability in terms of the interference of further methodological difficulties which simply need to be surmounted, firmly believing that the main obstacle to empirically capturing the intricacies of the treatment relationship and process is the need for an ever-more refined research technology. There are, however, more plausible reasons for the difficulties encountered by empirical research when it attempts to enter the field of treatment process and patient-therapist interaction.

At a general level, it can be argued that when you limit the research variables to what you can know, to the realm of conscious awareness, you radically distort the foundations of what makes the treatment process actually work. Limiting itself to what can be known through observation, empirical research omits all of that which is sensed, but remains largely unformulated. Stern (1997) has described this realm of cognition as a kind of mentation characterized by a lack of clarity and differentiation, "the uninterpreted form of . . . raw materials of conscious, reflective experience that may eventually be assigned verbal interpretations and thereby brought into articulate form. . . . The affective accompaniment ranges from playful interest to a sense of awe, dislocation, and disorientation so severe it can be nauseating. Among children, more rarely adults, fears sometimes shape the ambiguity, so that fright or terror results" (p. 37). This is a realm of experience which has a huge impact in the treatment process. The very attempt to specify this type of experience in an empirically nomothetic way results in its loss; it can only be retained through narrative accounts, the anecdotal case presentation where the experience is described *as best* as the person can. Hoffman (1992b) has similarly argued:

> The idea that individual case studies are [simply] hypothesis-generating whereas nomothetic empirical research is hypothesis-testing is a false dichotomy based on the assumption that there are more controls for contaminating variables in the systematic research situation. That assumption in my opinion is false. Some things are controlled for more (for example every patient gets the same questionnaire), but other things are controlled for less. In general terms what is not controlled for are the influences of qualities of particular patient-therapist dyads, and beyond that, qualities of particular moments of interaction of particular patients with particular therapists. (p. 4)

The distortion created by attempting to apply the empirical approach to the treatment process can be described in another, but related, manner. The position of the ideological empiricist demands certainty from the scientific evaluation of treatment. More realistic natural scientists acknowledge the Heisenberg principle of uncertainty, recognizing the very influence of observation upon the object of scrutiny. The idea of uncertainty, however, takes on another dimension in the therapeutic treatment process (Hoffman, 1992c, pp. 293-294; 1998). It becomes a *different kind* of uncertainty to the degree that the patient is not simply an object of observation, but more fundamentally an active *agent* in the process. To the extent this different kind of uncertainty is recognized as *indeterminacy*, the patient is recognized as an agent with the *freedom to act*, rather than simply as a passive object in the treatment process. This element of indeterminacy is also reflected in the very *nature* of discourse in the treatment dialogue. People speak with allusions, metaphors and approximations which defy the scientistic quest for certainty. Their very use of language is *often indeterminate* in the sense that it defies precise measurement, as when a patient feeling unhappy bemoans that they "have the blues" or are "feeling kind of low."

A second major area in which one can see the consequences of the power of positivistic or scientistic thinking is in its efforts to define the nature of psychotherapy in a reductionist manner, an approach which is almost completely dominant in virtually every aspect of mental health practice. The following discussion will describe one aspect of this effort, though it is only one of many ways that this mode of thinking is trying to change our understanding of how treatment should take place. One of the "findings" of the scientistic and managed care approach to the treatment process is that therapeutic change occurs in a particular sequence, and that changes *must* follow this pattern (Harvey & Harney, 1997; Howard, Lueger, Masling, & Martinovich, 1993). While this type of finding is used as one of the justifications for the time-limitations imposed by managed care upon the provision of mental health services, an examination of the assumptions upon which such findings rest raises serious doubts.

One of these suppositions refers to our conception of the nature of order, the assumption that any orderly system can be portrayed by predictability in a manner similar to the linear deterministic laws of classical physics. Aside from the objection that this type of predictability does not really apply to human psychology due to the complexity of the human mind, it has become clear that the orderly model of the world suggested by classical physics was largely an artifact of our own scientific selection. In recent years, we have seen this concept of order superseded by more complicated and realistic non-linear dynamics, such as chaos theory, catastrophe theory, and complexity theory (Galatzer-Levy, 1995; Seligman, 1996; Wolff, 1996a, b). At a more practical level, the methodology of empirical research requires the construction of certain artifacts, specifically the notions of a metaphoric "average patient" who is suffering from a precisely delineated "average disorder."

In the treatment setting, this "average patient" is then viewed as a more or less passive object for the application of standardized techniques defined for his/her "average disorder." The psychotherapy process, then, comes to be viewed simply as a matter of medical prescription, with a linear, expected course just like the antibiotic treatment of symptoms related to viral or bacterial infections (Hoffman, 1992b). The reference to "medical prescription" here is meant in a broader metaphorical sense. It is not intended as a denial of the fact that advances in psychopharmacology have indeed provided a variety of medications that have been found to be invaluable for the treatment of a number of psychological symptoms, and which also have the potential to have a beneficial effect upon the conduct of psychotherapy with patients. Of course, the integration of psychotherapy and psychopharmacology remains a new, but hopeful frontier.

But real patients in a real treatment relationship are not simply passive objects, but rather participate as *active agents.* As active agents, they present conflicts which fall beyond the realm of the application of symptom-related techniques. For example, patients need to *actively decide for themselves* to let go of certain ways of thinking, feeling and behaving. In other words, we might be able to empirically validate that a particular course of action will result in a particularly beneficial effect. But the patient's questions about whether they *should* in fact commit themselves to that course are beyond the field of empirical investigation. At this level of conflict, then, change depends less upon an empirically defined sequence than upon when and whether the patient decides to make certain choices. No amount of programmatic teaching about "coping skills" directed toward symptom reduction can provide the resolution of this kind of existential conflict (Hoffman, 1992b). Therefore, recognizing the patient as an active agent in the treatment process demands a perspective which differs radically from the outmoded linear scientistic model of predictable, orderly progression. From this view of the patient as an active participant, the course of therapy involves talking about what people with unrealized potentials, engaged in the creation of new choices in their lives, are likely to decide to do *over time.* It is a perspective which emphasizes the value of human decisions and freedom more than the illusion of empirical prediction.

A CRITICAL POSTSCRIPT:
BEYOND OBJECTIVISM IN MENTAL HEALTH CARE

The scientistic, managed care paradigm of the treatment process has had disastrous practical consequences for many patients suffering from the more chronic and severe emotional disturbances. Strupp and Binder (1984) long ago noted that short-term care is indicated for the *least* problematic cases. Patients with the more severe character disorders have traditionally been excluded from short-term therapies (Ursano, Sonnenberg, & Lazar, 1991; Gabbard, 1994). In particular, disorders which have proven to be relatively refractory to short-term, time limited treatment include narcissistic and borderline character disorders, certain types of depression (especially childhood depression), patients with histories of physical and sexual abuse, and patients presenting comorbid psychopathology.

Shapard (1997) has presented a number of case vignettes, illustrating the human toll of managed care's policy of restricting access to or delimiting the duration of mental health services. The limitations of managed care, rationalized by the scientistic treatment paradigm and driven by cost control policies, effectively exclude coverage for severe or chronic mental illness, with disastrous effects upon the most vulnerable patients. Shapard's vignettes describe the impact of the time-limited forced termination inherent in managed care guidelines upon patients with dissociative disorders, suicidal ideation, post-traumatic stress disorder, issues related to physical and sexual abuse, and preadolescent and adolescent emotional problems. Early terminations with these types of cases was too often associated with the emergence of regressive suicidal behavior, massive psychological decompensation resulting in a deterioration of health and work functioning, resumption of substance abuse and life-threatening sexual activities.

It is ironic that in this time of concern about managed care and reduced lengths of treatment for troubled children and adolescents in the United States, we are confronted in residential treatment with an ever larger number of children with chronic disturbances, most often children born in circumstances of urban social disorganization and personal despair, who are unable to profit from customary modes of intervention. Often psychologically damaged during early childhood, these children have been described as throw-away children, the children that no one wants. Too many professionals in the field of child welfare have concluded that these children suffer from primary attachment disorders and are unable to respond to remediation. Often unable to respond to short-term treatment approaches, they sometimes become incorrigible adults with often horrible criminal outcomes.

The effects of public policy aligned with managed care directives have had effects in the field of residential treatment which parallel the impacts upon mental health care in general. Traditional models of group care have come under attack as the scientist perspective of treatment has filtered down through the managed care climate and converged with a public policy about troubled children which emphasizes "permanency planning" and "family reunification" over the needs of some children for longer-term individual and milieu treatment. Within residential treatment, this has led to the managerial preoccupation with outcome research, some would say at the expense of a devoted attention to the theory and details of the clinical practice actually being conducted in residential treatment centers. In place of the clinically rich reports so prevalent during the earlier years of residential care, we have witnessed a rush to accommodate to the demands for shorter-term treatment models. Accordingly, painstaking psychodynamic treatment has given way to objectivist models relying upon "consequences" and "reinforcers" for behavior, forms of treatment which give little real credence to children's feelings, wishes, or motivations in their formal treatment protocols, since these phenomena cannot be easily counted or measured. We have also witnessed the proliferation of individual and group forms of treatment tailored specifically to particular symptomatic issues or interpersonal deficits (for example, "anger management" or "social skills enhancement"), as well as the popularization of short-cut treatment approaches, such as those which claim that in treatment of the effects of early physical or sexual trauma, the cathartic experience alone is sufficient for psychological recovery.

All of these shorter-term approaches avoid the kind of existential issues which so often fuel the intense behavioral disorders displayed by young people. This kind of issue was illustrated by one long-abandoned teenage boy's intense craving for mirroring attention, a gnawing fear that "no one in the world thinks I'm the most special one to them." It was this very existential issue which time and again drove the boy to explosive rages, outbursts which were impervious to behavioral methods, but which eventually responded to a psychodynamic, relational approach attuned to the boy's underlying needs (Zimmerman, 1999). Another example involved an adopted teenaged girl with a severe learning disability from a highly professional family, where the other siblings were considered to be geniuses, taking the fast-track to Ivy League schools. In her case, the symptoms included wild histrionic behaviors, sexual promiscuity, and finally a suicide gesture. The underlying issue was eventually revealed to be the girl's feeling that, in comparison to others in her family, she was "damaged goods." As in the previous case, behavioral consequences and rewards were no match for the accumulation of interactional moments in a long-term relational treatment approach, which enabled her to replace a degraded self-image with some conviction that she was a valuable person in her own right. But these moments were not simply an accumulation of therapeutic interventions which could have been "scientifically" predicted or sequentially planned from a treatment template. Nor were they defined as a search for the hidden truth about the girl's life; rather, they were part of a process characterized by the gradual emergence through an inquisitive acceptance of uncertainty, of ideas that may never have been thought before, the emergence over time of constructions that were essential parts of the interactional world of the girl and her therapist in a dialectical relationship with and within the interpersonal environment. Far from the notion of scientific certainty, new understandings such as these have something of the quality of "effective surprise," marked by the symbolization of unformulated experience as a kind of mystery. Stern (1997) describes this sometimes unexpected flowering of meaning:

> It provokes in us the feeling of recognition, the shock of recognition, because we have seen its outlines before—in parataxic, amorphous, felt form, in our feelings of tendency. . . We feel as though we had been looking through poorly focused binoculars without realizing it. Somehow the adjustment is made, and suddenly and unexpectedly, the view leaps out at us in fine detail. In just this way, by creating between them a world of thought and curiosity, patient and analyst rescue unformulated experience from the oblivion of the familiar. (p. 79)

The crucial issue in this part of the discussion is not simply that the shorter-term methods trivialize the critical existential issues in clinical practice. The objectivist theories underlying those methods also *mini-*

mize the very worth of *asking* the kinds of questions which motivated the early founders of residential care for children, because those questions were about inevitably indeterminate human qualities. Such inquiries included the question of how we might provide the best care for children, which necessarily led to the question of what do we need to attend to as children grow up, in turn leading to various theories about child development. There were the important questions explored by Aichhorn and Anna Freud about the impact of early attachments, and the possible long-term psychological effects of specific problems in those primary relationships. There were other important questions, such as Anna Freud's attempts to provide a framework for how we think about children's adaptive capacities, Fritz Redl's curiosities about how we might find better ways to deal with violently aggressive children or "the children who hate," and Bettelheim's attempts to understand the existential issues which seemed to be associated with childhood psychosis.

The issue of whether the conclusions reached by those pioneers were correct or not is of less importance in this discussion than the fact that they lived in a climate where such questions were taken seriously. And the danger of today's scientistic climate is the tendency to conclude that because the scientific method doesn't work for such questions, they are either unimportant or wrong. This rigid "pragmatism" of our time betrays a stunning lack of curiosity about the problems it cannot solve. It is a dangerous atmosphere which encourages facile, morally bankrupt responses to the sometimes unfathomable richness of the textures of human existence and culture. The scientistic dehumanization of human experience and culture has been perhaps nowhere more clearly indicated than in B. F. Skinner's (1953) proclamation that culture is no more than the accumulation of social reinforcement contingencies by a group, a pronouncement which has in recent times become the anthem for much of modern-day behaviorism. From this perspective, the values and intellectual achievements of a particular culture are reduced to the status of reflexive responses to environmental pressures. In this objectivist view of humans as no more than passive objects of environmental influences and manipulation, social contingencies, or the behaviors they generate, become the "ideas" of a culture, while the reinforcers that appear in the contingencies are said to be its "values." Extreme forms of objectivist "pragmatism" thus purport to offer yet another "final solution" to the problem of understanding humanity and culture, but instead, some might claim, it vacuously creates a barren caricature of culture, ignoring the complexity, depth, and darkness of human life.

On the other hand, staunch opponents of the more rigid forms of the objectivist perspective warn that individual freedom, will, choice, creativity and imagination are all ultimately in danger of succumbing to the exclusionary claims of this type of scientistic thinking. It is probably more reasonable, however, to resist absolutist views of the effects of social influence and post-modern convictions about social-embeddedness, as well as the belief that humans can function as totally autonomous agents. In other words, the experiential gap between social influence versus freedom seems rather to point to a conception of "relative freedom," where there is a recognition that even as "free agents," there is no ultimate resolution of the indeterminacies of life, either by ever-more careful attention to our "authentic selves" or by a dedication to discovering our "true aims" (Hoffman, 1998).

Rather than siding exclusively with either the claims of social influence or of total human freedom, a conception of "relative freedom" requires that we develop the capacities to create the most skillfully-crafted, well-informed syntheses we can create with regard to the decisions and choices we must make in the face of the ambiguities of life. To make a closely paraphrased extrapolation from Hoffman's observations about the dialectical-constructivist clinical perspective, it is a conception of agency which acknowledges that there are indeed both given known and unknown limitations to our sense of freedom. In this sense, it is acknowledged that human experience is essentially heterogeneous, and that we can never know, particularly in light of the many contingencies that are beyond our control, what it would have been like to follow the life courses not taken. The result of these factors, and others, is a sense of more or less acknowledged existential uncertainty, a sense of indeterminacy that accompanies whatever path is chosen, whatever decision is made, despite whatever degree of conviction we might bring to it. The responsibility to make choices in the context of irreducible uncertainty is highly disturbing. However, grasping at external guideposts for direction, whether beliefs in the ultimate effects of "social influence" or absolutist tenets about human insight or "freedom," probably serves mainly as a defense against the responsibilities we all face in making important choices for our own life actions (Hoffman, 1998, 25-26).

REFERENCES

Aichhorn, A. (1925/1965). *Wayward Youth* (Trans. E. Bryant, J. Deming, M. O'Neil Hawkins, G. Mohr, E. Mohr, H. Ross, & H. Thun). New York: The Viking Press.

Altman, N. (1993). Psychoanalysis and the urban poor. *Psychoanalytic Dialogues, 3* (1), 29-49.

Altman, N. (1995). *The Analyst in the Inner City: Race, Class, and Culture Through a Psychoanalytic Lens.* Hillsdale, NJ: The Analytic Press.

Bachrach, H. M., Galatzer-Levy, R., Skolnikoff, A., & Waldron, S. (1991). On the efficacy of psychoanalysis. *Journal of the American Psychoanalytic Association, 39,* 871-915.

Barrnett, R. J., Docherty, J. P., & Frommelt, G. M. (1991). A review of child psychotherapy research since 1963. *Journal of the American Academy of Child and Adolescent Psychiatry, 30* (1), 1-14.

Berger, L. S. (1995). Grunbaum's questionable interpretation of inanimate systems: History and context in physics. *Psychoanalytic Psychology, 12* (3), 439-449.

Bettelheim, B. (1955). *Truants from Life.* New York: Free Press.

Bettelheim, B. (1967). *The Empty Fortress.* New York: Free Press.

Bettelheim, B. & Sylvester, E. (1949a). Milieu therapy: Indications and illustrations. *Psychoanalytic Review, 36,* 54-68.

Bettelheim, B., & Sylvester, E. (1949b). Physical symptoms in emotionally disturbed children. *The Psychoanalytic Study of the Child, 4,* 353-368. New York: International Universities Press.

Bettelheim, B., & Sylvester, E. (1950). Delinquency and morality. *The Psychoanalytic Study of the Child, 5,* 329-342. New York: International Universities Press.

Blase, K. A., Fixsen, D. L., Freeborn, K., & Jaeger, D. (1989). The behavioral model. In Robert D. Lyman, Steven Prentice-Dunn, and Steward Gabel (Eds.), *Residential and Inpatient Treatment of Children and Adolescents,* 43-59. New York: Plenum Press.

Bolland, J., & Sandler, J. (1965). *The Hampstead Psychoanalytic Index.* New York: International Universities Press.

Bollas, C. (1987). *The Shadow of the Object. Psychoanalysis of the Unknown Thought.* New York: Columbia University Press.

Casey, R. J., & Berman, J. S. (1985). The outcome of psychotherapy with children. *Psychological Bulletin, 98,* 388-400.

Cohler, B. J., & Zimmerman, P. (1997). Youth in residential care: From war nursery to therapeutic milieu. *Psychoanalytic Study of the Child, 52,* 359-385. New Haven, CT/London: Yale University Press.

Cooper, S. (1993). Interpretive fallibility and the psychoanalytic dialogue. *Journal of the American Psychoanalytic Association, 41* (1), pp. 95-126.

Curry, J. F. (1986). Outcome studies of psychiatric hospitalization and residential treatment of youth: Conceptual and research implications. Paper presented at the 94th annual meeting of the American Psychological Association.

Curry, J. F. (1991). Outcome research on residential treatment: Implications and suggested directions. *American Journal of Orthopsychiatry, 61* (3), 348-357.

Curry, J. F. (1995). The current status of research in residential treatment. *Residential Treatment for Children & Youth, 12* (3), 1-17.

Ehrenberg, D. B. (1992). *The Intimate Edge. Extending the Reach of Psychoanalytic Interaction*. New York/London: Norton.

Eist, H. I. (1997). Managed care: Where did it come from? What does it do? How does it survive? What can be done about it? *Psychoanalytic Inquiry, 1997 Supplement*, 162-181.

Feynman, R. P. (1998). *The Meaning of It All*. Reading, Mass.: Addison-Wesley.

Fonagy, P., & Target, M. (1996). Outcome predictors in child analysis. *Journal of the American Psychoanalytic Association, 44* (1), 27-73.

Fonagy, P., & Target, M. (1997). The problem of outcome in child psychoanalysis: Contributions from the Anna Freud Centre. *Psychoanalytic Inquiry, 1997 Supplement*, 58-73.

Fourcher, L. A. (1996). The authority of logic and the logic of authority: The import of the Grunbaum debate for psychoanalytically informed psychotherapy. *Psychoanalytic Dialogues, 6* (4), 515-532.

Freud, A. (1941-45/1973). *The Writings of Anna Freud, Vol. III*, 1939-1945, 3-540. New York: International Universities Press.

Gabbard, G. (1994). *Psychodynamic Psychiatry in Clinical Practice: The DSM-IV Edition*. Washington, DC: American Psychiatric Association.

Galatzer-Levy, R. M. (1995). The rewards of research. In T. Shapiro & R. N. Emde (Eds.), *Research in Psychoanalysis: Process, Development, Outcome*. Madison, CT: International Universities Press.

Galatzer-Levy, R. M., & Cohler, B. (1990). The developmental psychology of the self: A new world view in psychoanalysis. *Annual of Psychoanalysis, 18*, 1-43.

Geha, R. (1993). Transferred fictions. *Psychoanalytic Dialogues, 3* (2), 209-243.

Gill, M. M. (1994). *Psychoanalysis in Transition*. Hillsdale, NJ: The Analytic Press.

Grunbaum, A. (1982). Can psychoanalytic theory be cogently tested "on the couch"? Part II. *Psychoanalysis and Contemporary Thought, 2*, 311-436.

Grunbaum, A. (1984). *The Foundations of Psychoanalysis: A Philosophical Critique*. Berkeley & Los Angeles: Univ. of California Press.

Grunbaum, A. (1988). Are hidden motives in psychoanalysis reasons but not causes of human conduct? In S. B. Messer, L. A. Sass, & R. L. Woolfolk (Eds.), *Hermeneutics and Psychological Theory: Interpretative Perspectives on Personality, Psychotherapy and Psychopathology*. New Brunswick, NJ: Rutgers Univ. Press, pp. 149-167.

Grunbaum, A. (1993). *Validation in the Clinical Theory of Psychoanalysis*. Madison, CT: International Universities Press.

Habermas, J. *Knowledge and Human Interests*. Trans. by J. J. Shapiro. Boston: Beacon Press.

Harvey, M. R., & Harney, P. A. (1997). Addressing the aftermath of interpersonal violence: The case for long-term care. *Psychoanalytic Inquiry, 1997 Supplement*, 29-44.

Hoffman, I. Z. (1992a). Expressive participation and psychoanalytic discipline. *Contemporary Psychoanalysis, 28*, 1-15.

Hoffman, I. Z. (1992b). Discussion of Ken Howard's paper at grand rounds at the University of Illinois, January 29, 1992. Unpublished manuscript, University of Illinois Medical School.

Hoffman, I. Z. (1992c). Some practical implications of a social-constructivist view of the psychoanalytic situation. *Psychoanalytic Dialogues, 2* (3), 287-304.

Hoffman, I. Z. (1994). Dialectical thinking and therapeutic action in the psychoanalytic process. *Psychoanalytic Quarterly, 63,* 187-218.

Hoffman, I. Z. (1998). *Ritual and Spontaneity in the Psychoanalytic Process.* Hillsdale, NJ/London: The Analytic Press.

Howard, K. I., Lueger, R. J., Maling, M. S., & Martinovich, Z. (1993). A phase model of psychotherapy outcome: Causal mediation of change. *Journal of Consulting and Clinical Psychology, 61* (4), 678-685.

Jacobson, L. (1996). The Grunbaum debate: Introduction. *Psychoanalytic Dialogues, 6* (4), 497-502.

Lear, J. (1998). *Open Minded: Working Out the Logic of the Soul.* Cambridge, MA/London: Harvard University Press.

Levenson, E. (1983). *The Ambiguity of Change. An Inquiry into the Nature of Psychoanalytic Reality.* New York: Basic Books.

Mitchell, S. A. (1988). *Relational Concepts in Psychoanalysis. An Integration.* Cambridge, MA/London: Harvard University Press.

Mitchell, S. A. (1997). *Influence & Autonomy in Psychoanalysis.* Hillsdale, NJ/London: The Analytic Press.

Nagel, T. (1995). *Other Minds: Critical Essays.* Oxford, UK: Oxford University Press.

Ogden, T. H. (1986). *The Matrix of the Mind: Object Relations and the Psychoanalytic Dialogue.* Northvale, NJ/London: Aronson.

Pfeiffer, S. I. (1989). Follow-up of children and adolescents treated in psychiatric facilities: A methodology review. *The Psychiatric Hospital, 20* (1), 15-20.

Pfeiffer, S. I., & Strzelecki, S. C. (1990). Inpatient treatment of children and adolescents: A review of outcome studies. *Journal of the American Academy of Child & Adolescent Psychiatry, 29* (6), 847-853.

Racker, H. (1968). *Transference and Countertransference.* New York: International Universities Press.

Redl, F., & Wineman, D. (1951). *Children Who Hate.* Glencoe, IL: The Free Press.

Redl, F., & Wineman, D. (1952). *Controls from Within.* Glencoe, IL: The Free Press.

Ricoeur, P. (1974). *The Conflict of Interpretations.* Evanston, IL: Northwestern University Press.

Sandler, J., Kennedy, H., & Tyson, R. (1980). *The Technique of Child Analysis: Discussions with Anna Freud.* London: Hogarth Press.

Schwartz, J. (1996). Physics, philosophy, psychoanalysis and ideology: On engaging with Adolph Grunbaum. *Psychoanalytic Dialogues, 6* (4), 503-513.

Searles, H. F. (1965). *Collected Papers on Schizophrenia and Related Subjects.* New York: International Universities Press.

Seligman, S. (1996). The irrelevance of infant observations for psychoanalysis: Response by Stephen Seligman. *Journal of the American Psychoanalytic Association, 44* (2), 430-446.

Shapard, B. (1997). The human toll: Managed care's restriction of access to mental health services. *Psychoanalytic Inquiry, 1997 Supplement,* 151-161.

Skinner, B. F. (1953). *Science and Human Behavior.* New York: Macmillan.

Small, R., Kennedy, K., & Bender, B. (1991). Critical issues for practice in residential treatment. *American Journal of Orthopsychiatry, 61* (3), 327-338.

Smith, M. L., Glass, G. V., & Miller, T. I. (1980). *Psychotherapy.* Baltimore, MD: Johns Hopkins University Press.

Spence, D. P. (1982). On some clinical implications of action language. *Journal of the American Psychoanalytic Association, 30* (1), 169-184.

Spence, D. P. (1983). Narrative persuasion. *Psychoanalysis and Contemporary Thought, 6* (3), 457-481.

Spezzano, C. (1993). A relational model of inquiry and truth: The place of psychoanalysis in human conversation. *Psychoanalytic Dialogues, 3* (2), 177-208.

Stern, D. B. (1997). *Unformulated Experience: From Dissociation to Imagination in Psychoanalysis.* Hillsdale, NJ/London: The Analytic Press.

Stolorow, R., & Atwood, G. (1992). *Contexts of Being. The Intersubjective Foundations of Psychological Life.* Hillsdale, NJ/London: The Analytic Press.

Strauss, L. (1953). *Natural Right and History.* Chicago: The University of Chicago Press.

Strupp, H., & Binder, J. (1984). *Psychotherapy in a New Key: A Guide to Time-Limited Dynamic Psychotherapy.* New York: Basic Books.

Tansey, M. J., & Burke, W. F. (1989). *Understanding Countertransference. From Projective Identification to Empathy.* Hillsdale, NJ: The Analytic Press.

Tramontana, M. G. (1980). Critical review of research on psychotherapy outcome with adolescents: 1967-1977. *Psychological Bulletin, 88,* 429-450.

Ursano, R., Sonnenberg, S., & Lazar, S. (1991). *Concise Guide to Psychodynamic Psychotherapy.* Washington, DC: American Psychiatric Association.

Voegelin, E. (1948). The origins of scientism. *Social Research, 15* (4), 462-494.

Voegelin, E. (1952). *The New Science of Politics.* Chicago: The University of Chicago Press.

Wolff, P. H. (1996a). The irrelevance of infant observations for psychoanalysis. *Journal of the American Psychoanalytic Association, 44* (2), 369-392.

Wolff, P. H. (1996b). The irrelevance of infant observations for psychoanalysis: Response by Peter H. Wolff. *Journal of the American Psychoanalytic Association, 44* (2), 464-474.

Wright, D. M., Moelis, I., & Pollack, L. J. (1976). The outcome of individual child psychotherapy: Increments at follow-up. *Journal of Child Psychology and Psychiatry, 17,* 275-285.

Zimmerman, D. P. (1990). Notes on the history of adolescent inpatient and residential treatment. *Adolescence, 25* (97), 9-38.

Zimmerman, D. P. (1999). Desperation and hope in the analysis of a "thrown-away" adolescent boy. *Psychoanalytic Psychology, 16* (2), 198-232.

Zimmerman, D. P., & Cohler, B. J. (1998). From disciplinary control to benign milieu in children's residential treatment. *Therapeutic Communities: The International Journal for Therapeutic & Supportive Organizations, 19* (2), 123-146.

The Little Turtle's Progress:
On Psychotherapy in Residential Treatment

D. Patrick Zimmerman, PsyD

SUMMARY. This article briefly discusses a number of arguments often given in support of the increased use of short-term residential treatment and examines some of the assumptions underlying those arguments. It then focusses upon the detailed description of an individual psychotherapy case study of a young child in long-term residential treatment. That case presentation indicates a number of clinical issues which appear to contraindicate the use of either brief therapy techniques or short-term residential treatment, and which also illustrate the need for the preservation of long-term residential treatment options for certain severely disturbed children and adolescents. *[Article copies available for a fee from The Haworth Document Delivery Service: 1-800-342-9678. E-mail address: <getinfo@haworthpressinc.com> Website: <http://www.Haworth Press.com>]*

KEYWORDS. Child psychotherapy, residential treatment, long-term psychotherapy

INTRODUCTION

For some time now, mental health professionals, public interest groups, child advocates, and others responsible for influencing the

An extended version of this article, entitled "The Little Turtle's Progress: A Reconsideration of the Short versus Long-Term Residential Treatment Controversy," was published earlier in *Children and Youth Services Review, 15,* 219-243, 1993. Copyright 1993, adapted with permission from Elsevier Science.

direction of child welfare national public policy have been pressing for, if not demanding, increasingly restrained, discriminating, and time-limited use of residential treatment for children and adolescents (Eisikovits & Schwartz, 1991; Hofmeister, 1990; Small, Kennedy, & Bender, 1991; Young, Dore, & Pappenfort, 1989). Some have proposed that one implication of this trend is that residential care as we have known it will cease to play a significant role in children's mental health services, and that it will no longer be viewed as an important component in the continuum of care in child mental health service systems (Eisikovits & Schwartz, 1991).

Some of the major pressure for the increased use of short-term residential treatment has come from the area of public policy, with its emphasis since the early 1970s on mental health de-institutionalization, and various notions about the use of the least restrictive environments in treatment (Small, Kennedy, & Bender, 1991; Wells, 1991a). However, both the large number of emotionally disturbed homeless adults who have been left to feebly fend for themselves on urban streets, as well as the startling increase in reports of the plight of physically and sexually abused youth, provide clear testimony to some of the most dismal failures resulting from the utopian, naive, and politically motivated claims of the de-institutionalization and "least-restrictive" movements. Associated with the movements promoting de-institutionalization and utilization of the "least restrictive" treatment environments has been an underlying suspicion about the residential treatment of children and adolescents (Wells, 1991a; Whittaker, 1990). Related to the public policy shift away from institutional care, and especially from long-term residential treatment, has been the economic concerns for fiscal constraints in mental health care, which have been accompanied by treatment time limits by both public and private third-party payers, and by demands for more accountable, cost-effective forms of treatment. As the economic concerns have become more intense, they have been accompanied by a history of legal controversies about the public responsibilities for the long-term residential care of children under existing federal special education legislation (Butler, 1988).

Another major influence in the attitudes which favor a movement away from the referral of children for longer-term residential care has been the growing enthusiasm about the efficacy of family treatment, associated with a perhaps overly-optimistic belief in its application to community-based care and the often utopian claims by proponents of family reunification programs. Some have proposed that this is a particular area where the public policy message is increasingly disconnected from the experience of clinical practice. In other words, the unambiguous policy message is that residential treatment programs should seek the permanent reunification of children and their families whenever and as soon as possible, but experienced clinicians have become more and more aware that "those of us immersed in everyday residential treatment practice see these same guidelines as less and less applicable to the real children and families with whom we work" (Small, Kennedy, & Bender, 1991). Another critical determinant in the movement away from longer-term residential treatment has been the perhaps uncritical embracing of the sometimes cult-like success claims of short-term or brief therapy, and the grafting or transplantation of those techniques onto the residential treatment program. It has been hard not to believe in an all-encompassing success for short-term treatment techniques, which have been heralded by their innovators and proponents as "the wave of the future" and a "twentieth century miracle" (Good, 1987; Malan, 1980; Strupp, 1980).

Despite the shift toward shorter-term group care for children and the use of time-limited therapy in the general field of mental health, a number of clinical issues appear to contraindicate the use of either brief therapy or short-term residential treatment for a number of severely disturbed young people. While it is beyond the scope of this article to discuss those issues in detail, reviews of this controversy have examined problems in the evaluative research (Zimmerman, 1993), as well as disturbing diagnostic concerns (Small, Kennedy, & Bender, 1991; Wells, 1991b; Wells & Whittington, 1993). Other commentaries have provided provocative discussions of the broader, underlying historical, social, scientific, and cultural assumptions which have propelled the acceptance of brief or short-term treatment (Good, 1987; Lear, 1998; Zimmerman, 1999).

Despite the reservations about the appropriateness of short-term care for many young people, we are faced with the paradox that at the very time that the calls for more limited time periods of residential treatment have become more strident, public agencies are referring the most desperately needy children for residential care (Small et al., 1991). Balcerzak (1991) reiterated this dilemma, when he pointed out that the children who are currently referred for residential treatment are clearly now more emotionally disturbed, have more extensive histories of failure and have dysfunctional to barely existent families, and yet there is a public demand to work with them in more time-limited and less intensive ways. It appears to be a public policy which almost guarantees the ultimate treatment failure for the growing numbers of these often profoundly impaired children and adolescents.

In light of the questions about the usefulness of short-term care or brief-therapy techniques for some children, the following selective report of a long-term psychoanalytically-oriented individual psychotherapy with a young boy in residential treatment may illustrate more richly the advantages, even necessity, of providing long-term opportunities for some types of severely disturbed children. As has been noted previously, this is of special importance since many practitioners have noted a trend in recent years of dramatically increasing numbers of referrals for residential placement of children with significantly more traumatic life histories and more severe levels of emotional disturbances.

THE LITTLE TURTLE'S PROGRESS

Over the years, there have been a number of approaches to child clinical material presentations. One common use of child case discussions has been to illustrate a particular developmental hypothesis, such as the drive or psychosexual, object-relations, or self-psychology developmental theories. This type of presentation often advocates the superiority of a particular developmental viewpoint, and seldom seriously questions whether there is real connection between the particular theoretical model presented and the actual treatment process as it unfolded between the therapist and child. A second major use of the presentation of child therapy case material has been to reconstruct the origins and dynamics of particular emotional child disturbances, such as obsessions, delinquency, childhood psychosis or schizophrenia, and, more recently, narcissism and borderline disorders. Again, these more focused descriptions of particular childhood pathologies have tended to be framed within specific developmental theories.

The purpose of the present case study of the long-term psychoanalytically-oriented individual psychotherapy of a young boy in residential treatment is neither to advocate a particular theory of child development, nor to focus solely upon a specific form of psychopathology.

Rather, the intent of presenting the following case material is to non-defensively illustrate selected aspects of the treatment process which appear to provide strong support for preserving long-term treatment opportunities for severely emotionally disturbed children and adolescents, despite the prevailing preferences for simpler, more directive, and shorter-term techniques. While this presentation of admittedly highly selective case material suggests a generally object-relations and transference-oriented treatment approach, strong efforts were made to avoid an overly technical descriptive approach in the overview of this particular six-year treatment relationship and the changes which seemed to occur during evolvement of that treatment process.

Background Information

Timmy entered residential treatment at the Sonia Shankman Orthogenic School at the University of Chicago when he was five years old. The treatment philosophy of the school is based upon long-term psychoanalytically-informed milieu therapy, which has been described elsewhere in a number of widely-read publications (Bettelheim, 1950, 1955, 1967, 1974; Bettelheim & Sylvester, 1947, 1948; Sanders, 1959). He was seen in twice-weekly individual psychotherapy for six years at the school, and during that time he was placed in a self-contained special education classroom and also received ongoing art therapy.

Timmy is the oldest of five siblings, with one younger sister and three younger brothers. The parents are well-educated, holding graduate degrees, and during much of Timmy's early childhood both parents worked in professional-level positions. Currently, the father is employed in a high-level position, but the mother no longer works outside the home.

Both parents have histories of significant loss in their backgrounds. Both of Timmy's father's parents died from cancer, his father when he was ten years old and his mother when he was in his early twenties. The father is preoccupied with work and driven to succeed, but he remains constantly worried that he could fail at any time. The mother's parents divorced when she was seven years old, and subsequent to that divorce she was placed in a series of foster homes. She remembers her childhood as a sometimes sordid one, a time of being frequently hit and spanked, surrounded by an atmosphere of divisiveness, fighting, and the near total absence of love. The opportunity for higher education, apparently, was her avenue of escape from this world, which she describes as having left her with life-long fears of abandonment. While Timmy's mother is clearly a woman of high intelligence, emotionally she appears to be driven, aggressive, and compulsive, although there is a strong sense of underlying disorganization. Over the years, she has consistently defended against her feelings of notable deficits in her child-rearing capacities with regard to Timmy through the use of intellectualization about the various sources of his emotional problems. Beneath her intellectualized approach to his emotional problems lies a vague suspicion that Timmy is inhabited by an incubus-like demon, which in later years could actually compel him to commit murderous acts.

Timmy's history of difficulties appear to go back to the very time of his birth, which the mother described as an exhausting ordeal. Timmy's mother suffered medical complications during the delivery, and subsequently spent the next ten days in intensive care. When she was released from the hospital, she felt too exhausted to attend to him, and a service agency was immediately called to send helpers into the home to care for him. Timmy's mother reported that from the very beginning, Timmy was a demanding baby and never seemed to sleep. Four months later, the mother returned to work, and during the next two succeeding years Timmy and two younger sibs (both born with medical problems) were cared for by a series of three child-care helpers. In general, the mother described feeling that she was relatively incapable of forming an attachment or bond with Timmy during his early years at home. Just before Timmy was two, his leg was broken when he fell after being "pulled" by the last of these helpers. He was hospitalized in traction for ten days and then was in a body cast for eight weeks. When he was three years old, he again suffered a broken femur when, according to the mother, she pulled him off a chair while he was dressing, in reaction to his continuing to "act up." By this time in his life, Timmy's mother had also begun to frequently spank him both with her hand and with sticks in driven, frantic efforts to control his impulsive behaviors.

Timmy began preschool before the age of three, but after the first two schools he attended found him already to be behaviorally unmanageable in their classroom settings, he was referred to a private child guidance clinic, which offered child therapy, a special education preschool class, and family counseling. Clinicians at this agency also almost immediately concluded that his behavior was unmanageable in even their very specialized, therapeutic setting, and they convinced the parents, especially in view of the admitted escalation of parental physical maltreatment of Timmy at home, to consider inpatient psychiatric hospitalization for him.

At even this early point in his developmental history, Timmy was observed to be easily over-stimulated, highly distractible, overactive, impulsive, and physically aggressive. He placed himself in situations of extreme physical danger to himself, such as calmly walking into oncoming traffic, and finally he was discovered on separate occasions to be trying to seriously injure two of his younger siblings. Both parents and clinicians at that point described his fears of the world and its invisible forces as fantastic, diffuse, and overwhelming; on the other hand, he was obsessed with ideas of aggression, violence, and physical assault upon others.

At the age of four, he was hospitalized for one year, and his parents received ongoing counseling at the hospital during the entire course of his inpatient care. Timmy appears to have made noticeable gains during the inpatient stay, especially in his ability to relate to adults in the hospital environment and to modulate his impulsivity and aggressiveness. Plans were made for re-unification with his family, but as soon as Timmy became aware of the impending discharge home, his functioning deteriorated rapidly and severely, exhibiting a magnitude of rage which staff members described as "murderous." Both the parents and the hospital clinicians immediately began to seek long-term residential care for him, and he was referred to the Orthogenic School shortly thereafter.

Psychiatric assessments of Timmy during the initial phase of residential treatment described him as a small, attractive child who initially tried to present himself to others in a pleasant, cute, and engaging way. However, it was observed that Timmy was still, in fact, severely emotionally disturbed, probably at a psychotic level of disorganization, but he was able to suppress the symptomatology and appear to function within a relatively normative range with the consistent supports of an institutional milieu structure. In other words, it appears that one thing he had managed to learn was how to hide his emotional illness, as he had done for much of his year-long inpatient hospitalization.

Nevertheless, Orthogenic School consultants cautioned, staff members needed to be aware that his reality testing was seriously impaired and that he was preoccupied with paranoid terrors of annihilation by monsters and demons, lurking invisibly within his everyday living environment, ready at any moment to leap out at him from behind walls or from within bathrooms and closets. Though he appeared to be clearly less flagrantly self-abusive than when he had lived at home, Timmy was still terribly preoccupied with ideas and concerns about bodily injury, on the one hand, and yet continued to engage in subtle masochistic and self-destructive gestures at the school. Described from another perspective, partly related to his history of physical maltreatment, Timmy had all kinds of fantasy and reality elements blended and mixed up with each other about who hurts whom, and how and why the infliction of such pain occurs.

From the foregoing description of Timmy's family history, a number of factors emerged which seemed to clearly contraindicate the potential success of either brief-therapy techniques or short-term residential treatment. The deficits in maternal attachment, Timmy's experiences of early and severe physical abuse, the failure of a number of increasingly protective treatment interventions, and the apparently broad-based and deep nature of his psychopathology all advocated for the clear need for a long-term, cohesively intensive residential living experience.

To Find the Words

Timmy began individual psychotherapy approximately one year after placement at the Orthogenic School, a usual practice which allows the child time to form significant relationships with a number of staff persons in the milieu. By the time he began individual treatment, his ability to repress his pathology in the general milieu had seriously eroded. Staff members, who some months earlier had questioned why this seemingly sweet and charming little boy was even in placement and remarked in consultations how he stood apart from the majority of our difficult to manage disturbed children, quite suddenly had come to view him as a demon and as some kind of monster-child. He provoked ongoing peer conflicts in his dormitory, had become emotionally explosive in both the dormitory and classroom, seemingly minor and subtle precipitants would quickly escalate to his expression of massive verbal and physical rage upon many staff persons who worked with him.

In sharp distinction to the image and increasingly rageful behavior he had come to display in the general school environment, during the first few weeks of individual therapy, and for periodic periods of time during the whole first year, Timmy would come to therapy and spend almost the whole session sitting stiffly and statue-like on the couch across from me, trying desperately to think of something to say. His attempts to talk would usually trail off with his murmuring, "I don't know what to say . . . I forget everything I could say." This ongoing seemingly massively repressed and amnesiac state would leave him appearing to feel profoundly distressed and depressed. Even though he knew there were toys in the room that he could play with or even just use to distract himself from his extreme discomfort, he would persist in sitting and desperately trying to find a way to relate to me by talking. For many weeks, no form of reassurance that I considered anything he might be able to come up with as valuable in his session facilitated his being able to talk or ameliorated his feelings of failure and depression in the face of this amnesiac-like state. This was clearly a type of child therapy which was from the very beginning in sharp contrast with the more active therapy, advocated by theorists and practitioners who depend heavily upon the examination and inter-pretation of the so-called transference meanings revealed through the child's active play and creative physical constructions in the therapy session.

I eventually came to sense that my own feelings of frustration, related in part both to my own feelings of being cut off from Timmy during these extended sessions of silence and to feeling inadequate in my efforts to facilitate any essential level of ongoing verbal interaction with him, may have been a reflection of the kind of frustration he had experienced in trying to establish emotional contact with his mother during his early years. Second, I began to understand his own feelings of failure and depression in those sessions as reflective of his own reactions to long-standing feelings of emotional abandonment by his mother (and fears of abandonment by his family related to the real precipitants of his hospitalization and subsequent residential place-ment). He was eventually able to tell me that he was terrified that because he wasn't able to talk, he wasn't "good enough" for sessions, and because of that I probably didn't want him in sessions and wanted to get rid of him. In a sense, then, the silences also came to suggest the possible direction of the unfolding of his transference feelings to me in the treatment process, namely, coalescing around maternal issues.

Eventually, at the beginning of one session, he was able to ask if I'd like for him to tell me a story. My response that I would indeed be interested in listening to his stories opened up a whole channel of creative, symbolic communication from him, which included story-telling, pretending to go to sleep and "making up" dreams, making up and singing operas in pseudo-foreign languages, and role-playing (including role-reversals, where he would be the doctor and I would be the patient–where he asked the questions and instructed me about what responses that I, as Timmy, should give). These forms of story-telling and role-play appeared to be a way for him to free-associate, while at the same time preserving a sense of structure to protect himself against the dangers of unmanageable levels of regression or fragmentation. They also, however, enabled him to slowly begin to peek out at the world from beneath his shell of repression.

Over the next few months, Timmy used these various forms of verbal play to convey to me a number of his most primitive fears and rages. For example, an early story illustrated his strong feelings of vulnerability from external threat, and also fears that the vulnerability to such danger might be contagious, when he told me a "scary" story about green, slimy, jelly-like monsters coming to get him (and probably me, too). This was succeeded in the next session by an elaboration of his strong oral needs for nurturance, which were co-mingled with rageful feelings toward his mother, through a long story about a peanut butter and jelly sandwich, out of which first came the green slimy monsters, and then his mother (from the "sticky," peanut-butter side of the sandwich). When his mother jumped out, he killed her. In the following session, he continued with this theme of murderous rage at his mother, telling a story in which his mother again appeared, but in a giant crowd of green, slimy monsters. In that story, Timmy became a knight, who then slayed his mother with a sword.

As the months proceeded, his stories told me about his fears that no one would help him, and that he felt that it was possibly his own fault (telling me the story of the boy who cried wolf, and ending it by looking down and quietly saying, "The boy in that story is me"). Periodically, then, he came to be able to tell a few simple dreams, which continued to emphasize the mixture of orality with fears of destruction, though now there came to be an element of hope: he dreamed of monsters and foxes . . . foxes eating . . . and a fox ate him, but he was finally able to escape through the fox's stomach. This sense of an emerging sense of hopefulness was also elaborated through song, as he sang me his own "compositions" about the sun rising on a happier day, and another about a man pushing the alarm button on a clock and all the people in the world would "wake up."

Other stories described his frustration at the seemingly endless task of coping with his emotional turmoil, leaving no time to enjoy life as a little boy, his painful sense of loneliness, his feelings of isolation from peers and siblings (and perhaps from me), and, again, feelings of optimism about the ultimate outcome of his suffering. These themes were clearly depicted in his story about the little boy with a blue ball. The boy was all alone on the outside of a house. He had to spend all of his time chasing the ball, which left him no time to actually play with it. Then, his "time was up" (metaphor for session ending, with an injunction that if I have expectations that therapy is only to do "work," it will drain his sessions of the possibility of childhood enjoyments). He then had to go back inside the house, where there were some other kids who asked him if he wanted to play with them. But he didn't want to, and told them, "No." He went back outside, and was all alone again . . . having to chase endlessly after the blue ball. Then he felt like he *did* want to play with someone. He went back inside the house, found the other kids, and ended up being able to play with them.

Other stories indicated that he was hopeful that the therapeutic relationship would help him deal with his feelings of fragmentation, anonymity, and lack of a true sense of self. He told me about a man named Zoo-Zoom (who, he confided, was really me), who was surrounded by thousands, millions, billions of little boys . . . all of them named Timmy T. Johnson. Zoo-Zoom had to find the real Timmy T. Johnson. He asked "What is your name?" of boy after boy. They each responded exactly the same, "Timmy T. Johnson." Finally, one said "Timmy T. Johnson" in a very *LOW* voice. And with that, Zoo-Zoom could tell, by the very low voice, that it was the *real* Timmy T. Johnson. This story also appeared to refer to his need to regard him as special, in spite of the presence of even "billions" of other little boys who might even look exactly like him. The fulfillment of similar wishes for mirroring admiration from me was also apparent in the great joy and delight he took in feeling that I appreciated, even enjoyed his many performances of original songs and improvised "operas" during the years of sessions.

Communicative Growth and Awareness of the Transference

During the second two-years of psychotherapy, a period hypothesized as a mid-phase, Timmy's verbal interactions with me turned
from the realm of the metaphoric to attempts to have more reality-
oriented talks with me. My therapeutic role during this phase emphasized efforts at clarification, helping him to extend and enrich what
began as simple reports of everyday conflicts and events, and eventually led to his being able to examine events in terms of precipitants,
sequences of actions and reactions, and the greater specification of his
emotional reactions to his daily experiences at the school.

Early oral phase cravings for nurturance and persisting fears of
abandonment continued to appear as themes in the material Timmy
presented during this phase. However, a number of other issues came
to the forefront, some of which represented the later psychosexual anal
phase of development: a growing interest in collecting things (stickers,
baseball cards, comic books), a plan to acquire a significant amount of
money by selling some of his old possessions door-to-door during one
of his extended home visits, and the struggle over gaining control over
his own impulses through playing checkers and backgammon with
me, where his aim was clearly more the growth and refinement of his
own ability to develop long-term strategies, rather than a driving competitiveness for victory over me.

A significant control issue between Timmy and me did develop,
however, within the treatment process and relationship. At one point
during this treatment phase, Timmy would start to tell me something,
and then, before continuing to actually describe or explain it in detail,
he would become demandingly insistent that I tell him if I had ever
done such a thing, or seen such a thing, or been to the place he was
wanting to talk about. I refrained from gratifying his need to know
even this limited amount of my personal reality, not wishing to rein-
force a dependence upon external support and direction in the area of
his growing communicative abilities. He reacted to this lack of revela-
tion on my part by repeatedly becoming enraged, and then lapsing into
a lethargic, depressed mood, claiming that he was no good because he
couldn't talk, and that meant, once again, that he wasn't good enough
for sessions and that I wanted to be rid of him. No amount of inquiry
about why he suddenly was feeling the need for such direct evidence
of support from me seemed to help. After many such episodes, howev-

er, I turned it all back to him with the comment, "Well, why don't you tell me about it just as *if* I *have* seen it, done it, or been there, too?" "Oh, yes!," he exclaimed, "*as if* you have!" And from that point on, he was able to resume his continued growing ability to express himself verbally.

Another area of great concern to Timmy during this phase involved the general issues of approval or disapproval, consequences of misbehavior and punishment. This concern about approval or disapproval was reflected in one way by a need to begin many sessions with a rather rigid accounting of his behavior, a rudimentary assessment of his feelings of self-esteem, at first in terms of whether he and his behavior in the dormitory and classroom in previous days had been categorically "good" or "bad." Over time, he developed an ability to review what he felt to be major behavioral incidents at the school not so much in terms of a primitive, moralistic judgment, but rather from a more sequential and dynamic perspective.

Somewhat associated with this, he was able to begin tentatively recalling incidents in the past with his parents. This was always a difficult path for him, and even through most of this phase, Timmy rejected any attempt on my part to offer a reconstructive interpretation, as distinguished from his growing ability to appreciate interventions focused upon our relationship in the here-and-now of the treatment process. He described feeling that focusing on his past would hinder his growth in the present, on the one hand, but also at that time he felt that if he talked openly about disappointment or anger toward his parents', he would jeopardize the possibility of actualizing his yearnings for a loving reunification with his parents and siblings in the future.

Nevertheless, as treatment progressed and he was able to feel more support from me in our relationship, he was able to begin saying things that he had previously been completely unable to talk about regarding his life at home. He reminisced about feeling unable to talk to either of his parents about things when he lived at home. Unable to talk to them, he said that he instead "acted them out," which only ended up with his getting hit a lot by both his mother and father. This left him feeling, he recalled, both angry and sad. Also, he was left with a profound sense of emotional confusion, because he "didn't know why they did it."

At this very time in treatment, and related to his discussions of punishment and prior experiences of physical abuse he began talking about being very interested in a comic book series based on a super-hero named The Punisher. He admired The Punisher, because he was very fair in the sense that he inflicted punishment strictly according to what a person had *done*, regardless of what kind of person they were, good *or* bad. At this point, Timmy found it surprising to consider that there might be a very different response to behavioral problems, to resolve conflicts arising from them by talking about them, rather than by resorting to punishment. Although he had heard staff members tell him about that alternative, it didn't mean anything to him until he heard it again in the context of his interest in The Punisher.

As this mid-phase of treatment came to a conclusion, Timmy began to make increasing derivative references to his transference feelings toward me as a maternal figure in the treatment relationship. For example, when his mother was again pregnant and he was anticipating the upcoming birth of a new sibling, at the beginning of one session he focused pointedly and with great surprise on his belief that I was suddenly getting "fatter" and, specifically, that it was mostly my stomach that seemed to be getting bigger. When I wondered if he wasn't perhaps seeing me as getting fatter because of his preoccupations with someone else getting fatter, he responded, "Yes, my mother."

A few months later, a playful over-dramatization appeared to convey to me both his wish to experience a sense of merger with me, as well, perhaps, as his symbiotic-like experience of the individual sessions at that point. He began by telling me that he had something *very* important to tell me. He talked about how he had been wanting to tell me, and *only me*, about this very important thing. Moreover, he had wanted to tell me for a *long* time, for years, since he was in his mother's womb. Yes, he continued, he had even wanted to meet me while he was still inside his mother's womb, before he was born, in order to tell me this very, very important thing. That ultimately there actually was *no* "important" thing to be told, also conveyed to me a clear message from Timmy that for *him*, the therapeutic *process* held much greater importance than the specific *content* of any particular therapeutic session.

A final observation should be made about the general picture of Timmy's behavioral functioning, emotional issues, and personality structure as this phase of treatment came to an end. In the treatment relationship, his communication skills, sense of self-esteem, and self-awareness seemed to have clearly improved. Staff members who worked with him in both the dormitory and classroom situations were finally reporting that, for the most part, his behavior had stabilized and he was once again regarded in a favorable way by those who worked with him. The psychiatric consultant also felt there had been an apparent shift in the symptomatic picture, with neurotic features having largely come to the forefront, in the place of Timmy's previously psychotic state.

Nevertheless, formal psychological testing revealed that reality testing impairments persisted, and that his underlying assumptions about object relations continued to be infused with malignancy and destructive aggression. In other words, at the end of this phase, there seemed to be a "sealing over" of the more serious pathology; formal assessment techniques suggested concerns that the seemingly greater sense of personal cohesiveness and calm that Timmy had appeared to achieve in his observable functioning in the milieu was perhaps quite tenuous and fragile.

The Final Years

The final two years of Timmy's therapy described here were typified by a continued burgeoning ability to reflect upon his emotions and communicate his feelings. His ability to make use of the therapeutic relational process became more sophisticated, partly reflected in his being able to communicate directly various aspects of his experience of the transference. As one example of his identification with the treatment process in the transference, Timmy came to session one day, laid down on the couch, and stated, "It's about the physiologist." "The physiologist?" I inquired. "Yes," Timmy replied, "you know, like you with the notepad, and I talk. And you're supposed to get a notepad and write down what I say." "You mean I'm to be the psychiatrist?," I asked. "Yes," Timmy replied, "the psychiatrist . . . now get your pad and write down what I say." What followed was Timmy's recounting a made-up nightmare of being pursued and physically threatened by one of his dormitory counselors, who was actually a demon disguised as a human. Of course, further examination of the fantasy dream revealed that it had a reality precipitant in Timmy's sensitive perception the evening before of one of his dormitory counselor's own ambivalence about and disagreement with a restriction he had to impose on Timmy for some misbehavior which had occurred the previous day, when a different dormitory counselor was on duty.

In a later session, I referred back to this incident and wondered to him whether his having me take the role of the physiologist-psychiatrist meant that he had been thinking more seriously of me in our relationship as a person who could help him with his problems. Timmy replied, "More like that you are my mind." "Your mind?" I wondered to him. "Yes, like thinking and remembering things." This referred, I think, to at least two important aspects of his growth and use of me in the transference. First, it indicated a growing awareness of the processes of his own mental functioning and expansion of his ego strengths and skills, and the representation of that awareness through projection of it onto me. Secondly, the description of me as "his mind" seemed to suggest his use of me in the transference as a container for his emerging sense of continuity, to which he could dependably turn when external stresses threatened him with feelings of fragmentation or regression.

Finally, in a later session, he described no longer feeling so much that I was "his mind." Instead, he said that he had come to feel like I was his mother. "Mother?" I asked. "Yes," he replied, "Like how I wish she had treated me when I was a little boy, and how I hope she'll treat me when I come back home to live." He then was puzzled about how he could feel that I, a man, could feel like a mother to him. This led him to consider how each of his parents acted toward him during his visits at home, and his feelings toward me became more understandable to him when he concluded that he had for some time experienced his father's interactions with him as more maternal than those with his mother, i.e., that his father was consistently more attentive, calm, and soothing, while his mother still tended to be more agitated, angry, and demanding with him.

As the end of this phase of treatment approached, Timmy was preoccupied with issues of going home, feeling that he was sufficiently into the process of growth to begin discussing the ways in which he felt he had changed over the years with his family. He also became determined to discuss with them what he felt were their distorted perceptions of him based on his past history, and to begin planning with them for his return home and the yearned-for reunification with his family members. This, of course, was accompanied by his telling a number of fantasy stories and "dreams" describing his worries and feelings of vulnerability related to those thoughts about returning home and having to face the demands of real life without the protective structure and dosed nurturance offered by the residential setting.

At the psychiatric consultations which reviewed Timmy's progress at the end of the six years of care reported in this presentation, it was concluded that he had become more able to tolerate increasingly greater affective stimulation and that he had developed a greater capacity to trust and to allow others to offer him comfort during times of unmanageable stress. He had resolved a number of pre-genital and oedipal issues, seemed to have developed a sense of morality with the beginnings of a healthier, less primitive, super-ego structure. He had become much less likely to withdraw into isolation and anger than in the past.

In addition, his treatment had revealed that there was an unusually healthy endowment in terms of talent, imagination, and relatedness that had previously been repressed by the extent of trauma and depth of emotional difficulties in his earlier life. Although it was expected that Timmy could continue to have periods of difficult regression in the community, it was felt that as Timmy matured he would continue to be able to access these healthier aspects of himself. Overall, it was felt that, depending somewhat upon the favorability of his family's living situation and the continued availability of outpatient psychotherapy resources, the prognosis for a successful, carefully planned transition to life outside of the school and reunification with his family was guardedly optimistic.

CONCLUSION

For some time now, there have been demands from a number of quarters for the increasingly restrained, discriminating, and time-limited use of residential treatment for children and adolescents. Some authors have even proposed that a major implication of this trend is that residential care as we have known it will cease to play a significant role in children's mental health services, and that it will no longer be viewed as an important component in the continuum of care in child mental health service systems.

The clinical presentation illustrated a number of clinical issues (including early childhood maternal attachment failures, previous treatment intervention failures, severity of psychopathology, significant communicative deficits, and particular characteristics related to the evolving treatment relationship), which appeared to contraindicate the efficacy of either brief therapy or short-term residential treatment for this type of case. Overall, the study attempted to unapologetically point to a number of persuasive reasons for believing in the need to preserve long-term residential treatment options for a number of severely emotionally disturbed children and adolescents, despite the prevailing preferences for simpler, more directive, and shorter-term techniques.

REFERENCES

Balcerzak, E. A. (1991). Toward the year 2000: Strategies for the field of residential group care. *Residential Treatment for Children & Youth, 8*(3), 57-70.

Bettelheim, B. (1950). *Love Is Not Enough*. New York: Free Press.

_____(1955). *Truants from Life*. New York: Free Press.

_____(1967). *The Empty Fortress*. New York: Free Press.

_____(1974). *A Home for the Heart*. New York: Alfred A. Knopf.

Bettelheim, B., & Sylvester, E. (1947). Therapeutic influence of the group on the individual. *American Journal of Orthopsychiatry, 17*, 684-692.

Bettelheim, B., & Sylvester, E. (1948). A therapeutic milieu. *American Journal of Orthopsychiatry, 18*, 191-206.

Butler, J. A. (1988). National special education programs as a vehicle for financing mental health services for children and youth. In *The Financing of Mental Health Services for Children and Adolescents: Papers Presented at a February 1988 Workshop*. Washington, DC: National Center for Education in Maternal and Child Health, 65-76.

Eisikovits, R. A. & Schwartz, I. M. (1991). The future of residential education and care. *Residential Treatment for Children & Youth, 8* (3), 5-19.

Good, P.R. (1987). Brief therapy in the age of reagapeutics. *American Journal of Orthopsychiatry, 57*(1), 6-11.

Hofmeister, J., Weiler, V. E., & Ackerson, L. M. (1990). Treatment outcome in a private-sector residential care program. *Hospital and Community Psychiatry, 40*, p. 927.

Lear, J. (1998). *Open Minded: Working Out the Logic of the Soul*. Cambridge, MA/London: Harvard University Press.

Malan, D. H. (1980). The most important development in psychotherapy since the discovery of the unconscious. In H. Davanloo (Ed.), *Short Term Dynamic Psychotherapy, 1* (pp. 13-23). New York: Aronson.

Sanders, J. (1989). *A Greenhouse for the Mind*. Chicago: University of Chicago Press.

Small, R., Kennedy, K., & Bender, B. (1991). Critical issues for practice in residential treatment: The view from within. *American Journal of Orthopsychiatry, 61*(3), 327-338.

Strupp, K. H. (1980). Problems of research. In N. Davanloo (Ed.), *Short-Term Dynamic Psychotherapy, 1*, pp. 379-392. New York: Aronson.

Wells, K. (1991a). Long-term residential treatment for children: Introduction. *American Journal of Orthopsychiatry, (61)* 3, 324-326.

Wells, K. (1991b). Placement of emotionally disturbed children in residential treatment: A review of placement criteria. *American Journal of Orthopsychiatry, (61)* 3, 339-347.

Wells, K., & Whittington, D. (1993). Characteristics of youths referred to residential treatment: Implications for program design. *Children and Youth Services Review, 15*, 195-217.

Whittaker, J. (1990). Challenges for residential treatment. Unpublished manuscript.

Young, T., Dore, M., & Pappenfort, D. (1989). Trends in residential group care 1966-1981. In E. Balcerzak (Ed.), *Group Care of Children* (pp. 11-35). Washington, DC: Child Welfare League of America, p. 12.

Zimmerman, D. P. (1993). The little turtle's progress: A reconsideration of the short versus long-term residential treatment controversy. *Children and Youth Services Review, 15*, 219-243.

Zimmerman, D. P. (1999). Scientism and managed care: The betrayal of group and individual treatment for children. *Therapeutic Communities: The International Journal for Therapeutic & Supportive Communities*, 20(4), 281-300.

Desperation and Hope in the Analysis of a "Thrown-Away" Adolescent Boy

D. Patrick Zimmerman, PsyD

SUMMARY. This paper presents a commentary on the analytic treatment of a depressed, highly agitated, and often rageful adolescent boy in residential care. Given the boy's ongoing experiences of desperation, an interactive analytic treatment perspective seems to have helped to foster his psychological growth and sense of optimism about the future. It was an approach which at varying times focussed on the discussion, symbolization, and enactment of massive, often overwhelming feelings of loss, misunderstanding, disappointment, and rage. From this persistent struggle in the face of despair, emerged a growing sense of hopefulness, wishes for intimate human connection and special feelings of attachment within the context of the here-and-now therapist-patient interactions. Over time, this adolescent boy became increasingly able to build a life founded upon "new experiences" of the world, a life which was in striking contrast to his traumatic, disappointing past. *[Article copies available for a fee from The Haworth Document Delivery Service: 1-800-342-9678. E-mail address: <getinfo@haworthpressinc.com> Website: <http://www.HaworthPress. com>]*

Earlier versions of this article were presented at the 17th Annual Meeting of the Division of Psychoanalysis (39), The American Psychological Association, February 28, 1997, Denver, Colorado, and at the 48th Annual Meeting of the American Association of Psychiatric Services for Children, March 26, 1997, New Orleans, LA. The author expresses appreciation to Irwin Z. Hoffman, PhD, and Bertram J. Cohler, PhD, for their valuable comments on this article. The author is also deeply indebted to the staff members of the Sonia Shankman Orthogenic School for their dedicated work, as well as to the members of the school's Board of Directors for their ongoing efforts to ensure the mission of the school. A version of this article was previously published in *Psychoanalytic Psychology, 16* (2), 198-232, 1999. Copyright 1999 by the Educational Publishing Foundation. Adapted with permission.

[Haworth co-indexing entry note]: "Desperation and Hope in the Analysis of a 'Thrown-Away' Adolescent Boy." Zimmerman, D. Patrick. Co-published simultaneously in *Residential Treatment for Children & Youth* (The Haworth Press, Inc.) Vol. 18, No. 2, 2000, pp. 107-143; and: *The Forsaken Child: Essays on Group Care and Individual Therapy* (D. Patrick Zimmerman) The Haworth Press, Inc., 2000, pp. 107-143. Single or multiple copies of this article are available for a fee from The Haworth Document Delivery Service [1-800-342-9678, 9:00 a.m. - 5:00 p.m. (EST). E-mail address: getinfo@haworthpressinc.com].

KEYWORDS. Residential treatment, psychoanalysis, adolescent psychoanalysis, social-constructivist

INTRODUCTION

In recent years, there have been few extended reports of analytic work with children and adolescents conducted in residential or group care settings. This may be due in part to current changes in the nature of residential care, including movements toward shorter-term treatment and the use of more directive cognitive and behavioral techniques. It may also reflect the observation that analytic treatment in group care has always been challenged and complicated by the presence of unusually intense and ubiquitous transference-countertransference issues which arise with respect to both the planned residential milieu and to the formal structure of the treatment facility (Bettelheim, 1974; Bleiberg, 1987; Borowitz, 1970; Ekstein, Wallerstein, & Mandelbaum, 1992; Levy, 1967; Rinsley, 1980), and that can have a direct influence upon the therapist's decisions and interventions (Zimmerman & Cohler, 1998). Nevertheless, it is important to remember that much of the early analytically-oriented work with youth was conducted in group care and residential centers. The present work represents an example of psychoanalytic work with children and adolescents in group settings, and is indebted to a tradition which began in Vienna (Aichhorn, 1925/1965, 1964; Freud, 1930/1973, 1941-45/1973; Freud & Burlingham, 1944/1973; Heller, 1992) and was later implemented in the United States during the period immediately following the Second World War (Bettelheim, 1950, 1955, 1967, 1974; Redl & Wineman, 1951, 1952).

The following clinical discussion of the analytic treatment with a depressed and highly agitated adolescent boy in residential care is a presentation of highly selective case material. Efforts were made to avoid an overly technical approach to the narrative of this treatment relationship and of the changes which seemed to occur during the evolvement of that treatment process. Too often, in published presentations of psychoanalytic cases, the clinical material is chosen as secondary illustrations for a preexisting conceptual scaffolding. For me as well, presenting this case ultimately led to making a choice between emphasizing a format that stressed the selection of material to illustrate particular examples of dialectical thinking and participation in the boy's treatment, and an organization which attempted to emphasize the tone of the ongoing development and progress of the treatment. Given the relative paucity of extended accounts of the analytic process with adolescents, especially from backgrounds of poverty and maltreatment, the case material here stresses the latter. Nevertheless, this choice was made with the hope that the reader would still be able to discern the strong interactive nature, conversational tone, and dialectical perspective which were always embedded as crucial elements of the ongoing treatment experience with this adolescent (Ghent, 1992, 1995; Gill, 1994; Hoffman, 1994, 1998; Mitchell, 1993, 1997; Pizer, 1992; Slavin, 1994).

STEVE'S EARLY LIFE:
THE FOUNDATION OF NOT BEING UNDERSTOOD

Steve entered residential treatment at the Sonia Shankman Orthogenic School at the University of Chicago when he was 13 years old. He was seen in individual treatment for three and one-half years at the school, twice weekly during his first year of therapy and four sessions of psychoanalysis per week thereafter. The treatment philosophy of the school was based upon analytically informed concepts of milieu therapy, which have been described in detail elsewhere (Bettelheim, 1950, 1955, 1967, 1974; Zimmerman, 1993). Steve had two older living sisters and one sister who was deceased. He had a traumatic childhood history, replete with extensive experiences of neglect, as well as physical and sexual abuse. Steve's father had worked briefly at manual labor, but approximately 3 years before Steve's birth he was diagnosed with schizophrenia. There were numerous inpatient psychiatric hospitalizations, and the father presently resides in a psychiatric facility. Steve's mother came to a large midwestern urban center from a small West-Coast town, "looking for the excitement of the big city." Family difficulties were clear even before Steve's birth. Reports had already been filed against Steve's father, accusing him of sexually molesting two of Steve's older sisters; police records also documented severe physical violence by the father against the mother and the oldest sister. When Steve was about 6 months of age, his mother separated from her husband and moved to California with her four children.

While in California, she became increasingly neglectful of the children, exposing them to her own promiscuous sexual activities, including alleged prostitution, and drug abuse. The children were frequently left alone for long periods of time, and they often had to go out and steal food from groceries and convenience stores to survive. Her physical abuse of all four children became increasingly unpredictable and violent. Finally, one evening (around a holiday period) Steve's oldest sister, unable or unwilling to suffer the continuing abuse, committed suicide by hanging herself. Steve had been left home alone the following morning and found his sister's body when he awoke, at first thinking that she was playing a holiday prank on him. It was only after she failed to respond to a playful smack from him that Steve realized with shock that she was dead. After his sister's suicide, Steve's father went to California and brought the remaining three children back to live with him in the Midwest, where they lived briefly in shelters and his car. Without resources for housing or food, the father eventually abandoned the children at the office of a state childcare agency. Steve was placed briefly in the care of an uncle, who sexually abused Steve in a particularly sadistic manner. Steve then went to live with an aunt and her husband. Steve's emotional state began to seriously deteriorate; his behavior became increasingly aggressive and explosive at home and in his public school setting, suicidal ideation was noted, and severe mood swings were observed. Eventually, Steve became a ward of the state, after which he had three inpatient psychiatric hospitalizations and two separate placements in a residential treatment center offering a behavior modification treatment approach. During this period of decompensation, Steve exhibited increasing verbal and aggressive behaviors, depression, and increasingly severe mood swings. He was variously diagnosed with bipolar disorder, depressive disorder, and attention-deficit hyperactivity disorder.

Psychopharmacological interventions prior to Steve's placement at the Orthogenic School were generally unsuccessful in containing his agitated rageful states, or in modifying his feelings of depression. Those treatment efforts included trials of Lithium, neuroleptics, and medications for anxiety, depression, and hyperactivity. After the third in-patient hospitalization, Steve was placed in residential treatment at the Sonia Shankman Orthogenic School. During his first two years of residential care at the Orthogenic School, Steve was treated (with variable results) with Lithium and then an anti-psychotic medication. At the beginning of Steve's second year in analysis, he had achieved some degree of control over his angry states and feelings of hopeless-ness; given the limited effectiveness of medication with Steve, the medical consultant decided to discontinue the use of medication.

INDIVIDUAL PSYCHOTHERAPY: THE FIRST YEAR

One of the first things that comes to my mind is how quickly Steve seemed to become engaged with both me and the idea of having individual psychotherapy sessions. There seemed to be a clear hunger for attachment. From the very beginning of the treatment relationship, he was able to talk freely with a wide range of emotions, including feelings of anger, warmth, and nostalgia about various aspects of his past. However, much of his early interaction with me involved my serving as an audience to his venting of rageful feelings of frustration and indignation about many of his interactions with peers and staff members at the school. Although the nature of his ongoing complaints often seemed to convey a glimpse into some of Steve's own underly-ing feelings of distress, Steve could only listen to interpretive inter-ventions in a passive, non-rejecting way. He was usually unable to actually engage in any real discussions of possible genetic issues, intrapsychic difficulties, or aspects of our interactions within the ses-sions that might have some association to his external interpersonal frustrations and conflicts, the minute behavioral examination of which often consumed a great deal of his energy in our relationship.

Steve began his sessions by giving me a brief historical account of his life before coming to the Orthogenic School. There were a number of lengthy gaps in this retelling of his life history. Nevertheless, some of the more significant aspects of his recollections to me were related to five major areas: a terse discussion of his biological mother, a brief reference to his father, discovering his sister's body after her suicide, living with his aunt and uncle, and his experiences at a previous residential school. Regarding his mother, Steve described her as hav-ing "a mattress taped to her back," referring to his memories of living with her in California, where he claimed she constantly brought differ-ent men into their trailer home to have sex. He also talked about her being on some kind of drug, he claimed not to know the specifics, and of her being physically (and impulsively) abusive and neglectful to-ward him and his sisters.

Some months later, after Steve had continued to refer to his mother as having "a mattress taped to her back," I wondered to him whether that one degrading picture of her wasn't perhaps in part a diversion from other feelings about her that he wasn't mentioning. He responded by saying, "Yes, if I ever meet up with her again, I'd want to kill her." Associating to his recollections of this neglect, Steve talked more about his sister's suicide. He described how he discovered her hanging, but approaching her from behind, he thought she was playing a joke and "swatted" at her body until she swung around and he saw that she was discolored and dead. He remembered that when he ran to get help, the male adult who came to the trailer ended up chastising Steve for slapping at his sister before realizing that she was dead.

During these months in treatment, Steve vaguely referred to his biological father a few times–at least twice suggesting that he'd like to see his father. However, he felt that either staff members wouldn't let his father visit or that, since his father might still have been homeless, staff members wouldn't know how to get in touch with him. As with the mother, Steve did not talk about any real hope that the father would ever be able to provide him with any guidance or support as he navigated the tasks of adolescence and young adulthood. If Steve looked for any familial support in those areas, when I first began sessions with him, he talked of the aunt (the father's sister) and uncle as potential resources. However, listening carefully to his musings about that wished-for "family" as he showed me pictures from their home, I rather quickly came to see that a great deal of his actual expressions of affectionate feelings were actually displaced upon the family dogs at home, rather than the actual people (his relatives).

As the months passed in session, talk about the aunt's home and the family members there nearly disappeared, and his discussions shifted almost entirely to his current interests, concerns, and conflicts related to his more immediate surroundings and interactions at the school. Specifically, his more animated discussions in sessions during the first six months tended to revolve around four main issues: barely hidden excitement over his pubertal biological-bodily changes, criticisms of younger dormmates, his competitiveness in physical recreation games and sports activities, and complaints about his counselors. Of these issues, I would like to focus first on his (acknowledged) competitiveness in physical activities, which often became a real problem in group activities and would result in Steve's being criticized for making peer activities quite difficult. Zaslow (1988) has described patients somewhat similar to Steve in their ability to recall and describe their histories of abuse right from the start of treatment. He described them as frequently hyperalert and hypersensitive, often with preoccupations with body image and intactness. They critiqued themselves and others mercilessly, often relating the abuse to their mothers, while viewing their fathers as indifferent or weak. For such patients, Zaslow proposed, no consistent helping images or relationships emerged from the past, except those which validated their observable performance and achievement, such as with Steve, through recognition of his remarkable athletic skills and prowess.

In such cases, the attempt to contemplate ideas of getting help can often lead to feelings of being left in a void; for such individuals, real change often may entail a therapeutic relationship not essentially characterized by the linking of problems with past events and current interpersonal relationships, regardless of how mutual or benign that activity might be viewed by both participants in the treatment setting. In addition to Zaslow's (1988) observations, I often tended to understand Steve's intense athletic competitiveness variously as expressions of his sense of grandiosity and omnipotence, of attempts to satisfy early ungratified wishes for admiration, and of externalized needs for internal control. However, suggesting those possibilities as ways to look at what was going on in his very competitive playing, and the interpersonal conflicts it often aroused, was usually only met with compliant skepticism. He listened, but being actively introspective about his own internal processes seemed to be a relatively unwelcome prospect to him for many months.

At that point in the treatment, it was difficult to discern whether my interpretations to Steve served any useful function for him at all, whether related to some form of drive gratification, superego demands, reality demands, recollection of early internalized object relations, or the maintenance of self-cohesion and self-esteem. What was more clear was a seeming lack of any real associative response on his part to my interpretive activity. At any rate, this seeming impasse raised an important question for me in the treatment relationship. Specifically, I began to wonder whether Steve's present discussions of problems in his current life could be viewed simply through the more classical prism of repetition activity, or whether they should be understood from the more reparative perspective of his attempting to have a *new* kind of experience in his relationship with me, regardless of the seeming similarities between his current behaviors and his more chronic difficulties.

It was only some months later that I was able to see what seemed to be a more important therapeutic activity for Steve than interpretation. As an atmosphere of open-mindedness emerged in our relationship, a new kind of play, very different from his intensely driven and competitive athletic play, became an important arena for the treatment, creating new possibilities of experience in the life of this seriously traumatized and deadly serious boy. Many examples of play which are described in this paper could be understood in ways similar to some of Altman's (1997) hypotheses about the *interaction* between interpretation and play. It is important to note that the often interactive play approach with Steve frequently departed from the classical view of play as primarily focussed upon repression and symbolization, theories which emphasize that the therapist's participation or involvement is mainly in the service of decoding children's unconscious lives through themes, conflicts and symbols embedded in the play. Rather, although acknowledging that children's play does have a representational quality, work with Steve demonstrated that often the very process of playing, or "just playing," had a therapeutic effect. Neubauer (1993) has similarly proposed that it is possible for play to facilitate psychological growth without interpretation. From an ego psychology perspective, he suggested that during play the defense of displacement is at work in a way which allows conflicts to be "re-placed" onto symbolic objects, whereby the ego achieves increased mastery over them. From a more interactional viewpoint, "just playing" for Steve appeared to meet some of his intense early needs for attunement, empathy, and mirroring admiration from an adult caretaker. At such times, therapist involvement as an active participant came to the foreground, and the role of interpreter of latent meanings took its place in the background of the often mutual play activity. As playing moved more into the forefront of treatment, Steve slowly began to test new modes of relating with me and became more able to speak to me in his own language, often sensual and erotic, with tenderness and passion.

Another issue involved his heated complaints about his dormmates and staff members. Whenever his dormitory would have even a brief episode of argumentation or chaos, although Steve was often an active participant and at times the major provocateur, he would become enraged, leave the dormitory and storm around the school while venting his impassioned criticisms of his dormmate's behaviors. I frequently thought of his inability to tolerate even minor disruptions in the dormitory as related to associations to the chaos and unpredictability of his early childhood, as well as to the very real tragedies which ensued. With regard to his indictments of staff persons, his vehement complaints tended to center around very particular themes: They misunderstood him, they did not treat him according to his developmental-age needs, they failed to be consistent in their decisions, and they suddenly and unpredictably shifted their attention away from him to others in the dorm, leaving him with a sense of feeling abandoned in terms of their interest in him. Steve needed to have a sense that the adults working with him were in almost perfect attunement with his feelings and needs. Anything less than that resulted in feelings of painful injury, leading to his verbal outbursts against the adult.

One example of his rage against staff members for their lack of exact attunement with his needs involved his baseball skills. Steve was keeping a tally one summer of the number of homeruns he could hit over the outfield wall, and one day he erupted into an extremely aggressive verbal rage at the male counselor who was pitching to him. Investigation of the incident revealed that the precipitant was that Steve had felt that the counselor was not pitching the balls to him in the absolutely exact, perfect way he needed in order to hit the ball over the fence. Moreover, as the "perfect pitch" continued to fail to materialize, Steve began to become suspicious that the counselor was not simply failing to match his very precise needs as a good batter, but that he was, moreover, doing it on purpose to thwart Steve's need to prove that he could hit such long home runs.

Aside from the issue of attunement, Steve's view of the game may also have both preoedipal and oedipal implications. Although some readers might see these different perspectives as dichotomous, the counterposition to this objection is that different perspectives, such as relational versus intrapsychic or preoedipal versus oedipal, are intrinsic to and always present in the analytic situation; sometimes the one, sometimes the other is in the foreground, often depending on the analyst's focus (Gill, 1993; Hoffman, 1991). Accordingly, looking at the baseball incident from an oedipal perspective, Steve was playing with the staff person as though the baseball, even the whole game, belonged to him. Phillips (1997) has discussed a similar game activity as a metaphor for the oedipal struggle to recognize relational triangulation and its rules. From Phillips' perspective, the stance Steve took toward the counselor and the baseball in their game might well have reflected the manner with which he was dealing with issues of the Oedipus complex; he was living as though the object belonged to him. Steve appeared to be asserting the preoedipal rule that fathers (the male counselor) are obligated to affirm the child's absolute claim to rights over the mother (in this instance, the baseball). This sense of omnipotence also signaled some denial of the complications of the Oedipus complex. Writing about omnipotence as an opposition to engaging in the struggles of oedipal conflict, Phillips proposed, "that there is no such thing as omnipotence, that it does not exist in anyone, is the central and daunting and liberating acknowledgment at the heart of the Oedipal complex" (1997, p. 748).

From another perspective, while the counselor was offering a mutual activity, Steve was intent on preserving the game as baseball for one with another (ancillary) person. On the one hand, Steve was denying the reality of a three-person, triangular relationship in the game in favor of a two-person relationship (him and the baseball), but even this two-person configuration was shadowed by a one-person, self-relationship, since he basically defined the overall activity as baseball for one (himself). It was part of Steve's struggles in treatment to move forward from a precarious two-person relationship mode to the even more vulnerable triangular or three-person conception of relationships, rather than to retreat even more to a reliance upon his one-person relationship position.

Similar complaints about his sense of a lack of attunement from adult care-takers were frequently the precipitants of his blow-ups in the dormitory. In my own mind, Steve's sensitivity and rages against his counselors' thoughts and distractions seemed to resonate with one of his early major experiences of oedipal triangulation–between him, his mother, and the "other" in her own mind, represented by her own thoughts and distractions. In that experience, his rivalry and loss to the other were associated with his traumatic abuse and abandonment. It was not entirely surprising, then, that in his present life at the school the lack of attunement was associated with his perception of the other in his counselors' minds, represented either by their views that differed from his own or by their thoughts about other children. The catastrophic potential of recognizing the reality of this triangular relationship again in the present would lead Steve to strident denials of its validity. This opposition to the three-person experience usually involved retreat to rageful omnipotence and to a strenuous denial of the validity or worth of the world of the other in his counselors' minds, dismissing the logic of their reasoning or attacking their thoughts about other children as unnecessary, misguided, or further evidence of their deliberate intentions to ignore and mistreat him.

At one point, I wondered to him whether his great sensitivity to his counselors' thoughts and behaviors didn't have some parallels to what he had described to me about his mother: that he felt she hadn't met his needs–even the basic ones of providing food, that she was inconsistent and unpredictable (even to the point of exploding into physical abuse with no apparent warning signs), and that he felt she constantly shifted her attention away from him and his siblings, to the numerous men with whom she got involved. Steve was able to see the parallel, but the impact for him of the more immediate replay of these themes in the dormitory (in his eyes) far outweighed the significance of recognizing possible genetic links–at least at this point in our therapeutic work. Further, he abruptly dismissed my curiosity about whether his descriptions of arguments with staff members in the dorm might also reflect similar concerns about me–that I would ultimately prove to be unable to understand him and provide a sense of predictable, dependable care in the therapy. For Steve, metaphor was a pale, undramatic, and seemingly ineffectual rival to the vivid experiences, however conflictual and painful, of his everyday life.

During his next six-months in therapy, Steve had an especially difficult time at the school, especially in his dormitory. In part precipitated by a series of staff departures in both his dormitory and classroom, he continued to spend most of his sessions vehemently complaining about feeling a lack of attention and support by staff at the school, of finding life with his younger dormmates chaotic and intolerable, and of feeling hopeless that his living situation would ever improve. His behavioral reactions to all of this, specifically in the dormitory, were extremely volatile, with long-lasting periods of intense anger. These outbursts were viewed by staff members to be potentially seriously dangerous to himself or to others. Often, partly understood by him as a way to avoid actually physically hurting others, Steve would leave the dormitory, and sometimes the school building itself, until he was able to regain some measure of self-control over his feelings of distress and volatility. In the long run, this use of escape as a defense against the potentially destructive effects of his rage was not effective, and his behavior continued to deteriorate, resulting in two brief psychiatric hospitalizations. The second hospitalization occurred shortly after the leaving of another of Steve's dormitory counselors, to whom Steve had become, in his own hostile-dependent manner, quite attached.

Subsequent to that second hospitalization, there was a noticeably positive shift in Steve's behavior and attitude about the school and the staff members who were working with him, as well as a change in his demeanor in our sessions. This seemed to be related to a synthesis of two experiences: (a) during his second hospitalization, Steve spent a great deal of time in relative solitude, writing the beginning of a highly detailed autobiography in an attempt to exert some sense of self-control and mastery over his traumatic early-life experiences, and (b) this effort appeared to predispose him to highly value his reunion with me and his counselors as persons, unlike those from his past, who were striving to be consistently available for him. In sessions, he returned from the hospital talking about feeling openly glad to be back; there was, for the first time, an explicit wish to be at the school. Further, for the most part, Steve's complaints about staff members and other students began to diminish. When he did complain, it was without the firm conviction he previously held that others were simply bad objects. For example, after he was moved into a different dormitory with more age-similar peers, he began complaining that he wished he was living back in his old dorm with his younger dormmates. I reminded him of how bitterly he had talked about the younger boys during the previous months, and went on to wonder whether this might be an example of how even when he got what he struggled for, in this case a move to another dorm, it never seemed satisfying. He responded, differently than he would have in the past, with a sense of bemused acknowledgement that this comment seemed plausible to him–but that he still should have a chance to visit with his former dormmates regularly.

In addition to this change from a generally irritated, complaining mood in sessions, there was a shift to an often largely nonverbal mode of relating to me; this did not seem to represent what some might describe as a regression in his ability to relate, but rather it appeared to be a shift to sharing his feelings seemingly without the need for words. Steve continued to greatly anticipate the time we spent together in sessions. He spent a noticeable amount of his time in session laying quietly on the couch, gazing at me with a somewhat childlike sense of longing. At these times, his look seemed to convey not only an intense fondness, but also a profound sense of yearning and sadness. At the same time, he took great pleasure in teasing me about what a "dork" and "dweeb" I was, often playing with the stuffed animals and having them join him in this seeming disparagement of me. He appeared to derive a great sense of glee in this play, this fond teasing engagement with me. It was tempting to understand this disparagement in terms of oedipal rivalry, a barely disguised wish to exercise humiliating power over me, by picturing me as a belittled, pitiful figure. However, this raised other questions, and there are probably more. Was this an example of his own overly-punitive superego, projected onto me as invitation for a punitive response to his insults? In a related way, did the disparagement of me stem from his own unbearable sense of being socially inept, unacceptable, and pitiful, that he needed to put into me? The more important issue, however, seemed to be how I would take this interaction. When I accepted it with a sense of humor, Steve in turn conveyed the sense that his teasing was really one aspect of his tentative efforts to experience a sense of safe intimacy and affection with an adult, which had been largely unavailable to him during childhood.

UNPACKING SELECTED ANALYTIC MOMENTS

Soon Steve began asking, indeed pleading, for more frequent sessions. Subsequent to my obtaining formal consultation regarding his request, I offered to increase the number of his sessions to four times a week, and explained the change from psychotherapy to analysis. The increase in frequency was associated with the emergence of a treatment process which met both the intrinsic and extrinsic criteria of a formal psychoanalysis (Gill, 1994, pp. 61-77). Steve's immediate associations about the increased number of sessions seemed to be very directly expressive of feelings of greater personal hope about a future for himself, of the possibility of finding more adaptive channels for his contentious nature, and in particular of wishes to make reparation for his previously disruptive behavior in the milieu. For example, he began talking about wanting to stay at the school until he graduated from high school and could consider going to college. He mused about how his argumentative, detail-minded tendencies might actually be quite useful if he became a lawyer. Even here, however, Steve's preoccupations with the precariousness of relationships seemed to predominate–he especially didn't want to be a criminal lawyer (their cases are too "nasty"), but he was attracted to the idea of working as a divorce lawyer. Later, he talked about wanting to make a real contribution to the school's student Christmas show, by reciting a poem about devotion to and caring for others, as well as by presenting a puppet show act, with an "endearing" puppet he had made and named "O.S." (Orthogenic School). He followed through with these plans, and in session expressed a degree of self-pleasure that rivaled the pride with which he previously reported his admirable athletic achievements. The act of sharing began to be openly acknowledged by Steve as a possible source of feelings of self-worth, a source which was quite different from his accustomed mode of aggressive, intensely competitive sports activity.

As the analysis continued, Steve became increasingly playful, both with objects and with fantasy stories. His play began to reflect an ascendance of increasingly mutual and creative feelings, and some diminishment of his earlier preoccupations with themes of difference, rivalry, and triumph. One of his first "invented games" involved a set of small plastic cowboys and Indians, with their horses. At first, the game centered around arranging all of the horses with their rear ends pointed at me, and then they would all "fart" at me. This expression of anal aggressiveness toward me as an oedipal figure provided Steve with immense feelings of glee (given that his own father had been a ghost figure in his life, and too sick now to be the real target of such hostility). However, the game was soon transformed into an exhibition of Steve's fine-motor agility, when he built a precariously tall, free-standing tower with the horses and human figures–still a phallic configuration, but metaphorically expressive to me of his wish to achieve psychic balance. He took such self-pride in his balancing achievement that he asked me for permission to leave the tower standing until our next meeting.

Another illustration of his communication through play involved the use of intersubjective, creative verbal fantasy. The session material reported here also reflects the sometimes quite noticeable erotic tone of his discourse, play, and transference feelings toward me. Further, it provides a convincing example of how the sexual, sensual, or eroticized transference may have many meanings (in this case the repetition of the sexually charged atmosphere of early life experiences with his mother, wishes regarding me, feelings about the therapeutic relationship as potentially capable of transforming of his earlier eroticized life experiences, the atmosphere of our sessions, and the residential milieu in general), in addition to the *manifest* sexual one (Klein, 1969; Lachmann, 1994). One day, Steve came into the session, lay on the couch, and announced that he and I were "going out." "Where are we going?" I asked. "Oh, to a really fun place, you'll like it a lot!" Steve responded in mischievous tone. Then, with a sense of great excitement, Steve fantasied about how he and I would go out to a nightclub that he owned, "Steve's Rock and Roll Club."

The club featured female dancers on stage–topless and bottomless (and, he assured me, that didn't mean that the tops and bottoms of their bodies were missing, but that they were nude dancers). Of course, Steve mused, there are many nude dance clubs in America, but his was very, very special. And because it was so special, he and I would have the best of times there. "How is Steve's Rock and Roll Club so different?" I asked. He responded that it was unique because everyone could "relate" to each other–the patrons could "relate" to the nude dancers on stage, but, more important, the patrons, especially he and I, could also "relate" to each other. Our trip to Steve's Rock and Roll Club lasted for two sessions, and in the second session Steve decided to build additions to the club, so that his patrons would never really have to go back home. It would become an interconnected mall-like structure, providing for many of our needs, not just for relating and attachment. After the nightclub closed we would go to "Steve's Restaurant" (for nourishment-nurturance), then to the health and fitness club, then drop our party clothes off at "Steve's Laundry and Dry Cleaners" (even if we partied together all night, we had to keep ourselves clean and respectable-looking), and then we would finally retire for a good day's sleep at "Steve's Motel" before returning to the Rock and Roll Club the next night.

Another example of his multi-faceted communication through play involved some battery-operated motors, batteries, small light bulbs and erector set parts that he brought to session some weeks later. He wanted to make the "fastest motors" and "brightest lights" that I'd ever seen. As he worked at constructing the various light and motor gadgets, he engaged in the following commentary toward me, which could hardly, among other things, be a less direct appeal for me to function as a soothing, admiring, mirroring self-object for him. "Watch me, watch me . . . you'll think I'm such a genius. Now I'm going to make this great light switch . . . Steve's switch . . . you're gonna' love this, you're gonna' love this. And now I'm going to make the awesomest 'thingamadigger' . . . 'thingamadicker' . . . a motorized propeller with a switch. And this is the wire connecting to the battery. . . . connecting wire . . . stick this wire right up your butt." The latter eroticized part of his associations could be understood from a number of perspectives: once again as an expression of wishes for connection and attachment, of aggressive sexual feelings, and of the possible or potential fusion of both those wishes. Further, the "connecting wire" may well have been an allusion to the actual sexual abuse he suffered in childhood, which did in fact involve the application of electrical shocks to his genitals.

With regard to the issue of interpretation in the treatment relationship, a great deal of the focus and evolvement in this area related to Steve's experiences of staff leavings, separations, and feelings of loss. In the earlier psychotherapy phase, leavings precipitated a degree of rage in Steve which necessitated one of his brief hospitalizations. Some months after this, I was away for a week-long scheduled vacation. In the session after my return, he spent much of the hour laying quietly on the couch. When I noticed a sudden minute flinching of his body, I inquired about what had been passing through his mind. He responded that suddenly the image had come to his mind of a classmate accidentally getting his head hurt some weeks before, and of how much the boy had bled. Steve was curious about why that image had come to him at that moment. I suggested that perhaps I had hurt him by being away for so long, despite the fact that it had been scheduled and announced to him far in advance. He lay quietly on the couch for the remainder of the session.

The following week, I had to miss a session, which I rescheduled for later in the week. Nevertheless, on the night of the missed session, Steve left his dormitory in a rage, because his counselor and he had gotten into an argument, and during the disagreement she had changed her definition of the word *touching* (she claimed he had inappropriately "touched" a dormmate; Steve claimed to simply have "brushed against" him). I suggested that he had gotten enraged when his counselor didn't stick by her "word," and wondered if his anger wasn't

partly derived from my not sticking by my word about regular sessions–having recently taken a week off, and then having to reschedule
a session. He denied such a connection, indicating that at that point he
was resistant to making such extra-transference connections and that a
more useful comment from me would have involved a more direct
approach, focussing my interest much more explicitly upon how my
actions were impacting him.

Not long after this session, two administrators announced that they
were leaving the school. He was enraged in our subsequent session,
going through the list of adults who had worked with him, and who
had left the school. Finally, he became engrossed in building a tall,
elaborate tower out of dominoes, and then made it come crashing
down. I wondered to him whether the announcement of these people
leaving had made him feel like things at the school were crashing
down around him. Steve responded that he hated it when "everyone
tries to make things psychological." I admitted that, although I didn't
interpret often, when I did, it was hard to phrase things for him. Would
it have been better, I asked, just to have said, "It reminds me of things
crashing down around you?" He responded, "Yes, that's better, it's
different." In other words, a more simple phrase like "speaking of
things crashing down!" was more acceptable to Steve, because it
referred directly to comparable situations, whereas my earlier intervention was more in the realm of allusion and latent meaning, which
Steve tended to resist. This interchange seemed to underscore the
importance of keeping close to the immediate experience, or of stay-
ing within the metaphor in responding to the play of children and
adolescents (Spiegel, 1994). Later in the session, responding to my
willingness to modify the interpretation, Steve stated that "life is
bad." When I asked about what things in life were bad, he replied,
"inconsistency."

As the session came to an end, Steve began to pantomime himself
"blowing up" and exploding, somewhat playfully conveying how
"things crashing down" and inconsistencies in his life made him feel.
Subsequent to this interchange, Steve spent the next week writing a
continuation of the autobiography he had begun during his second
hospitalization, and used his session hours to read me his detailed
writing. It appeared that he was responding to the fractures in his
cosmic order at the school by trying to find a sense of organization
through the construction of his own autobiography, in which he both

attempted to create a sense of continuity about his life, while at the same time telling me about all of his own preceding discontinuities in life.

The next week, Steve came into session talking angrily about a discussion he had the previous night with a counselor, after which Steve had briefly left the dormitory. Steve was angry because the counselor "always tried to talk psychological, to talk like a psychiatrist." He went on to say that this reminded him of the hospital, where "they all talked like that," leaving him feeling that they didn't really understand him. I asked him if he could tell me more about talking "too psychological," to which he responded, "like from a textbook, not from experience." In other words, to be meaningful to him, Steve was telling me that interpretations had to feel as though they were based in the realm of authentic interpersonal experiences, rather than upon psychological theory. This might also imply that affective forms of insight were of greater importance to Steve than interventions aimed at promoting largely cognitive forms of insight.

As the weeks went on, Steve began to have significant problems during the weekends, when I was away from the school. The school's administration asked me to begin carrying a pager on the weekends, so that I could be contacted and be more immediately available in the effort to calm him down during these periods of extreme distress. Finally, after one particularly explosive weekend outburst, I made the following interpretive intervention with him: "It has become increasingly apparent that your sometimes physical explosiveness (toward property) is consistently occurring during the days that I am away from the school, when we don't meet for sessions. There *is* a relationship between your feelings of violence and my being away from you. Further, your explosiveness is a direct attack upon me–that I shouldn't have any days off and should be here with you seven days a week. When I'm not, I get called, so it's a way to make me have you on my mind, and to make me feel guilty about not being able to be here to calm your rages. And *I'm* angry about these physical outbursts–they're destructive to you, to the environment, and to me–and I want you to *stop*."

I appealed to Steve's athletic and game skills, suggesting that learning to stop his rages might involve something like the strengths he demonstrated in athletics and other games, where the unpredictable represented a challenge to be successfully surmounted. Not that ingenuity prevents bad things from happening, but that it could help him to overcome bad things, including the feelings of loss and abandonment that my being away on the weekends seemed to arouse in him. He did not reject my interpretive comments, which were quite direct and stern; to have offered less, I felt, would have been to collude in regarding his explosive behavior as expectable, rather than as a place to deal with a pathological way of attempting to manage feelings of separation and loss. Subsequent to that intervention, the weekend rampages diminished, and I no longer had to be paged to help deal with his behavior.

In the weeks after that intervention, Steve gave indications of beginning to experience a shift in his experience of events in his everyday life. He was able to tolerate the leaving of another counselor without experiencing his previous states of anger and explosiveness. He spent a subsequent session hour drawing; whereas his drawings during the first year of therapy were obsessive, symmetrical red and black abstracts, now he drew a realistic still life picture of an apple illuminated by a lamp–a creative effort which was both more object-related, and also metaphoric. It suggested some increased capacity for understanding and for delay: One might speculate that he was beginning to feel like the apple of his mother's eye, where in the picture he was the apple and I might have been "the light." In a later session, Steve brought a large rocket that he had assembled for me to see and admire, again with potential metaphoric meanings: feelings of "taking off" in life, phallic exhibitionism in the sense of beginning to feel freer to show his power and energy.

HOPE IN THE FACE OF DESPAIR

In the following year of analysis, Steve's sessions tended to focus most often upon issues related to wishes for attachment and involvement with me, the importance of athletic performance to him, psychological growth and moves toward autonomy, his expressions of sexuality and aggression, and hopes for eventual reunification with his aunt and uncle, whom he continued to view as potential surrogate parents. During this time, however, that yearning for an eventual family life in the outside world was temporarily shattered, and his attempts to cope with that loss, with accompanying feelings of being thrown into an abyss with no safety net, often severely tested his confidence in the progress he had been making. His metaphoric "rocket" of renewed power and freedom sometimes seemed fated to have an aborted take-off. Further, his sense of crisis, despair and desperation in turn intensified my own struggles in trying to find the optimal balance between spontaneity, support, and direction, versus a stance of more "analytic" restraint.

It is important at this point to provide some detail of what occurred with relation to his hopes to someday return to live as part of his relatives' family. During a meeting with his publicly-appointed guardian, she told him that, in terms of his legal rights, after his next birthday, he could decide whether he wanted to remain in residential care, or whether he wanted to return home to live with his relatives. Unfortunately, despite the benign intentions of keeping him informed of his legal rights, the guardian had failed to confirm beforehand the possibility of whether the relatives were willing to assume responsibility for Steve, or bring him home. This unforeseen incursion of reality into the treatment setting, and into Steve's individual treatment, came to have a heightened ongoing impact on our work together for many months.

Even before this incident, Steve had already voiced suspicions to me that his relatives really didn't want him, a message that he read from their unwillingness to have him home for more than two days during school vacation periods. Ironically, during that time Steve alluded to some identification with Dennis Rodman, the maverick Chicago Bull's basketball player, perhaps aligning himself both with the need to achieve some recognition and also with Rodman's adopted status. Regarding the latter, however, Steve was pessimistic, announcing to me one day, "Nobody thinks *I'm* the most important [person] to them." It is also possible that one meaning of this desolate statement referred to a paradox within our treatment relationship. His statement may have been, as Pizer (1996) observed with one of his patients, simultaneously a sad protest at what was not between us in reality, but also an affirmation of what was between us in the treatment relationship. In other words, it was perhaps to some degree just because he felt special to me within the symbolism of the treatment space that he could complain that I might not really think he was the most important person in my life.

I already knew that his relatives were adamant about not taking him back home permanently, but decided not to be the messenger bearing that news. I took this position after considerable inner struggle, worrying that he wouldn't want to hear the facts from me or at all, but also wanting him to find out on his own as part of the process of coming up with his own plans. He spent more than a month waiting to hear more details about whether he could go home, and during that time I felt (and stated to him) that my primary help to him was to "hold" him with relative comfort in our sessions together while he got through this time of vagueness and ambiguity about going home. This period, and for some months after, tended to be characterized by an absence of rich association and metaphor, which had been so evident during earlier phases of the treatment. Steve's preoccupations with the dilemmas in his outside real world often left me feeling inadequate, that I wasn't able to take a more interpretive stance in my wish to be of help to him. Finally, during a summer 2-day visit to his aunt's home, his relatives made it clear to him that he couldn't come to live with them (explaining that they were too old and also were having financial problems). Returning to school and our sessions, Steve's immediate reaction to having his fears about their rejection of him confirmed was one of flight: He declared that right after his 17th birthday, he'd go to court and have himself declared emancipated, get a job and apartment, and live on his own. This proposed, somewhat impulsive course of action was maintained only briefly, to be followed by some denial of the rejection he had experienced: Once again he talked of going home to live with his relatives, enrolling in a special education school, and then going to college. However, then he realized that even if he could convince his relatives to take him back, they had no money for college. There seemed to be no safety net for his future.

During the subsequent extended process of the loss of hope for an eventual reunion with his relatives and movement towards an acceptance of that loss, other issues continued to be of importance, though often under the influence of this overarching issue of family rejection. These issues included accentuated complaints about staff members who were working with him, reactions to staff leavings, some increase in his feelings of anger, allusions to feelings of progress and growth, and expressions of needs for attachment and greater interaction with me during this time of distress. His increased wishes for a sense of interaction with me included his request for us to have a special time to play together, wanting to have "an hour of fun." Elsewhere, Price (1994) has written of the difficulty some deprived children have in their capacity to play, describing the emergence of play as crucially dependent on the availability of a facilitating early experience with the mother. Altman (1997) has proposed that

> When play is blocked or a child's activity is too concrete or driven, one hopes to facilitate [in therapy] that suffusion of the external world with the internal, psychic world that constitutes play. Play provides a psychic space in which the child's and the therapist's psyches can meet and join in a creative process. (p. 727)

Even though the active play of a growing, athletic adolescent involved spaces outside of the session room, I agreed to spend some time with him this way, and it led to a series of valuable experiences outside of the session room. As discussed earlier in this article, with Steve it was often clear that the very process of playing, or "just playing," had a therapeutic effect. At such times, my own engagement as an active participant came to the foreground, while my role as interpreter of latent meanings took a place in the background of our often mutual play activity. Although our play experiences could be seen as deviations from the traditionally understood analytic frame, they were also experiences which demonstrated the potential usefulness of action in the treatment process (Hoffman, 1994). Altman (1997) has similarly reported on his experience of playing basketball with a nine-year-old boy as an important therapeutic medium. Commenting on ways in which the concept of the Oedipus complex could be useful in post-classical psychoanalysis, Altman's (1997) article described the use of basketball games to foster a boy's integration of pre-oedipal grandiosity into an oedipally competitive mode, which empowered the boy without forfeiting the analyst's position as an adult in relation to the child.

Basically, Steve's "times of fun" with me took the form of two activities: playing basketball in the gymnasium and shooting pool in the school's playroom. Playing basketball with Steve consisted mostly of his demonstrating for me his considerable athletic prowess and shooting skills in his favorite sport, an opportunity which allowed me to provide him with a non-competitive mirroring admiration of his talents. Shooting pool provided a variety of experiences: some of the times we played were clearly competitively aggressive, and I was able to find ways to provide him with support and praise for his performance whether he won or lost in the competition. He tended to be overly disappointed and critical of himself when he missed a shot or lost a game, which gave me a chance to interpret in action how overly-punitive he could be toward himself at times, a super-ego difficulty which in fact extended into many facets of his life. Over time, the edge of competitiveness gave way to a sense of happy playfulness, sometimes combined with a friendly man-to-man camaraderie in our interactions around the game. In that sense, our play seemed to provide Steve with a temporary, playful experience of the feeling of "becoming a man," which adolescence entails for boys of Steve's age.

Within the session room, there were other forms of interactive play. Showing me his skill at juggling with foam rubber "coosh-balls," Steve delighted in turning his wish for my admiration of his skill into a mutual juggling routine, fostering his feelings of attachment through this playful engagement. Another time, he brought a puppet he had made to session, and announced that it was "Bubba." Recognizing the name from the movie, *Forrest Gump*, I replied, "Oh, a friend in need . . . something like me?" "Yep," he replied. Bubba was, of course, both of us, as he demonstrated the next day when he described how in the dormitory he had dressed "Bubba" up to look like Dennis Rodman (Steve's own basketball identification). At another time, after we had a disagreement about our views of his reactions to a particular problem, Steve initiated a re-visit for both of us to his imaginary "rock and roll club"–perhaps in an effort to gain reassurance that the differing views hadn't meant that we were no longer in mutual, close interaction with each other.

During this phase, Steve engaged in another form of play, an involvement in constructing houses, machines, and games. For certain holidays, he built large and elaborately decorated houses and dioramas-symbolizing for him the importance of holiday rituals associated with a wished-for sense of family. At another time, he became engrossed in making perpetual motion machines out of wood, scraps, and a small battery-operated motor. One could suspect that the self-perpetuating machine was, to some extent, reflective of some accommodation of the fact that he was in many ways on his own, and of the hope that he could learn how to become self-sufficient. These constructions were followed by Steve's creation of a huge version of the game "Clue." It consisted of a detailed map of a three-story house which extended some 60 square feet upon his dormitory floor, along with his own invented rules (winning meant getting through all the rooms of the house up to the attic, and eventually leaving the house from a window in the attic–the only window in the house). The house could have been a metaphor for the school as home–he liked the fact that the house had only one window, protected from external reality, in a sense representing the protective structure offered to him by the school.

Aside from the many forms of play during this phase, our conversations often touched upon his expressions of intense anger in the general milieu. Over and over, Steve would explode in the environment when he felt that staff members weren't understanding him, paying attention to his every need, or devoting their full attention to him when he needed them in the dormitory. His sensitivity to the loss of adults in his early life only fueled the sense of entitlement and justification he seemed to feel about his angry outbursts. Eventually, I came to understand his ongoing and adamant complaints about staff members' alleged lack of care as a special kind of protest, reflective of a desperate hope that things could be better for him in the present, that he need not be doomed to reliving the abuse and abandonment of his past. Following this shift in my own thinking about his complaints, coming to a different view, Steve and I were able to begin examining the difficulties he had in seeing that people can have differing points of view about the same situation, and that the differences were not necessarily mutually exclusive and could be tolerated. As noted earlier in this article, part of Steve's difficulty in tolerating differing viewpoints stemmed from his reluctance to recognize the complexities of oedipal triangulation, his inability to acknowledge that he did not own the other and the other's thoughts and views, to accept that the other person may have his or her own valid views and has the right to have thoughts about others. The struggle, then, became to help Steve realize that there was, even for him, such a thing as a triangle of people with their own thoughts and views, each of whom may be equally real and valid to himself or herself (Phillips, 1997). This examination of the issue of differing viewpoints, and attempts to understand and modify Steve's angry reactions to opinions different from his own, continued to be a part of our work to the very end.

In addition to being able to bring his extreme anger under some examination, Steve made progress in a number of other areas, not the least of which was his ability to recognize that there could be some days which did not necessarily contain the seed of imminent catastrophe. I am reminded of his whispering quietly to me on one occasion (when we were engaged in seemingly innocuous play activity), "Life is alright . . . a little bit . . . sometimes. . . . " "You mean things are going well for you lately?" I asked. "Yes," Steve replied. Similarly, a few days later as we were coming back from his dormitory where he had been showing me his huge construction of the "Clue" game, he muttered, "Nothin' much going on . . . ." "Nothing much?" I asked. "Yeah . . . no real problems lately, everything's been going okay."

A striking example of Steve's focus upon wishes for growth, and his feeling that he had achieved some real psychological growth, was communicated through verbal fantasy around the theme of treatment. One day Steve came into the session room, lay on the couch, and declared, "Let's play psychoanalysis, and you ask me questions." "Okay, but questions about what?" I inquired, a bit puzzled. "Oh, I'll pretend I had a dream, and I'll tell you about it, and then you ask me questions." "Okay," I agreed. "Well," Steve responded, "I had this dream that there are a million identical guys under dark water, and then there's something above like an inner-tube, with a bright light in the center, and then one guy goes up through the tube and gets slapped. Ask me questions about it, okay." Not terribly quick in my thinking, I asked, "A million identical guys? And where are you?" "Ask more questions, *more*," Steve replied. "A tube?," I asked. "Yes," Steve answered jokingly, "a great big 32-inch television picture tube." With great glee, he then told me it was about a baby being born and then slapped by the doctor, a "dream" as a possible allegory for his own issues of rebirth as an emerging adult.

A TRANSITIONAL PAUSE: CREATIVE GESTURES

Some months later, Steve began discussing wishes for more normative living and educational experiences than could be provided in his present residential school setting. Along with his publicly appointed guardian and his state welfare worker, he began investigating the possibility of once again living in a foster care placement. Those wishes, his planning efforts, and his eventual move to a community living setting raised issues related to termination, a closing phase, or perhaps more accurately in this case, a transitional pause in Steve's treatment. The term *pause* is perhaps more accurate than termination, because the public guardian, the child welfare agency worker, and

Steve had all requested that I continue seeing Steve after he moved into the community, to provide support to him during the experiences of transition to community life. I agreed to continue seeing him, after a one-month break, on a twice-a-week outpatient psychotherapy basis.

Sadness and Hope in a Good-Enough Good-Bye

Movement toward termination with Steve began shortly after his 17th birthday. As stated earlier, the beginnings of this phase were quite complicated, and settling the details of his leaving required an extended period of negotiations involving the school's administration, the prospective foster parents, staff members from the state public guardian's office, and workers from the state child welfare agency. The process aroused a number of mixed and troubling feelings for me. Initially, Steve began talking about generally feeling better emotionally. However, he noted that he was also beginning to feel somewhat "claustrophobic" in the highly structured residential setting and increasingly wanted to have more normalized school activities, such as taking classes outside of the Orthogenic School. I offered to advocate for his wishes for increased outside educational and social activities.

At the same time that Steve was telling me that he was feeling better, I learned that he was telling the school's Director that he was feeling depressed and hopeless. Further, in a meeting with his child welfare worker, he had stated that he wanted a chance to live in a foster home, rather than continue in residential care. In a following session, I presented the seeming paradox to him, noting that with me he had been talking about feeling better and that he had seemed relieved with my offer to advocate for increased outside activities to enrich his residential experience. On the other hand, I observed to him, he was presenting an entirely different picture to some other people–of feeling depressed and wanting to move on to foster care. He responded with some equivocation, stating "I didn't mean I want to go to a foster home *tomorrow.* I just feel like I can't get what I want . . . outside things, like classes at the university laboratory school, volunteering at bake sales, going to dances. Things like that." I responded that I still didn't understand why he was beginning to press his child welfare worker for foster care, in light of the fact that I had talked with the school's director about him taking regular classes outside the residential setting, and that the response had been supportive of his wishes. At this point, I felt that Steve had betrayed me and my efforts on his behalf, raising the unsettling issue for me of "aren't I good enough?" In our next session, I raised one of my reactions, stating that "It seems as though my offer to advocate for you wasn't good enough." Steve responded that "There's nobody to talk to here now. I can't really talk to the counselors, to my teacher, or to the administrators." "I'm not enough any more?" I asked. "Well, it's just so frustrating that I can't talk to anyone else," Steve answered.

The following week, Steve had a scheduled meeting with his public guardian. In a session before that meeting, I asked Steve what he planned to discuss with her. He said that he just wanted to talk with her about doing "more outside things," not about leaving the residential facility. However, at that meeting the public guardian introduced Steve to a man who was quite interested in having Steve come to live with his family. Almost immediately, plans were initiated for Steve to begin weekend visits with that family, and discussions began about when Steve might ultimately go to live there (allowing for a treatment closing phase of three to four months). The suddenness of all this caused a great deal of conflict and tension for me. Of course, I wanted to support Steve's efforts at greater independence and a chance to experience a version of good family life. On the other hand, I had my worries about such a precipitous move. Ultimately, I resolved to bring some of those feelings into my work with Steve, from the belief that the best care-giving I could offer him involved more than my best feelings or wishes for him (e.g., unquestioned support for his strivings), but rather an expression of the tension it created for me, that on the one hand I was supportive, but on the other hand I had my doubts. In fact, it seemed that Steve also was trying to cope with tensions about our relationship, within the changing context of leaving the school and becoming part of a new family.

As his weekend visits began, Steve had increasing difficulty talking about the good times he seemed to be having on his visits. I finally noted to him that his approach to me in our sessions had become increasingly "sheepish" after each visit, and that I could use his help on this. For my part, I told him, "I am feeling in a competitive situation, feeling a sense of rivalry with this new prospective family. And I'm reacting, I think, by sometimes being too skeptical of how it might work out, and at other times by being not skeptical enough." Parenthetically, reframing this situation for myself in terms of triangulation or oedipal issues helped restore a sense of balance. From this perspective, the sense of rivalry gave way to an awareness that while there is a clear value to endorsing the other parent, here the new family, acceptance of that value doesn't necessarily take away the right to doubt or criticize.

After confiding that I was coping with my own feelings of discomfort with this transition, Steve became noticeably more open in discussions of his experiences during the weekly visits with the prospective foster-family, and of his plans and feelings about leaving the school and analysis. With regard to the details of his weekend visits into the new community setting, Steve began to present a picture that was less idealized and more realistic. He began to react to his new objects in terms of many of his older concerns, complaining that the new parental figures weren't as responsible or caring for him as they could be. Again, he complained about not being listened to, that they sometimes acted as though they didn't want to hear or value his point of view. However, unlike earlier phases of treatment, Steve was more able to delay his reactions to these perceived failures in attunement from significant others. He had come to be able to consciously "stand aside" from his urge to act impulsively at those times, in favor of coping with his frustrations by trying to understand others' behaviors in a psychological way. He also became able to speak more openly of feeling exhausted and overwhelmed by the process, though without the strong feelings of depression he had experienced at times early in the treatment. Periodically, Steve expressed a growing dissatisfaction with his current counselors in the dormitory, focussing upon his opinion that they were disorganized and that there was lack of clear planning in the dormitory. This complaint was perhaps a displacement of his frustrations with the complexities of the ongoing negotiations between various outside agency personnel trying to work out the details of his transition to foster care. In any case, unlike during periods of distress early in his care at the school, Steve was now able to vent his dissatisfactions and criticisms within our sessions, without becoming overly disruptive within either the classroom or the dormitory environments.

As his leaving date became finalized, Steve entered a phase of review, a time when he seemed to become clearly more peacefully subdued. He began to recollect and become nostalgic about all of the people who had taken care of him during the years at the school. Staff members, even those with whom he had often been in rageful conflict, were recalled in great detail, with a clear sense of forgiveness. Though he still at times characterized some staff members' past interactions with him as illogical and "goofy," he became more and more able to acknowledge the irrationality of his own rageful outbursts against property at the school during his early years. For example, when he stated that the counselors were sometimes "goofy," I asked, "And *you?*" "Oh, me?" he responded with laughter and a sense of humorous self-criticism about memories of his earlier rageful outbursts, "Crash! Oh, I'm sorry . . . oops, crash. . . oops, boom . . . oooohh, I'm sorry!" Following this joking reminiscence about his early behavior at the school, Steve quietly stated that he really wanted to come back to the school someday to be a counselor, perhaps an expression of identification with me, a process that others have described as an important route through omnipotence and oedipal dilemmas (Altman, 1997; Phillips, 1997).

Steve also talked about the girlfriends with whom he had been involved during his many years in residential care, specifically focusing upon the intensity of his feelings for each one and the emotional devastation which followed each of those separations or losses. As an indication of the emergence of the capacity for self-inquiry, Steve went on to tell me that as he thought about each of these girlfriends, he realized that in each case they had come to "carry other feelings for [me] from the past and from whatever present living situation I happened to be in . . . then, when the relationship would end, all of those feelings would come pouring back out all over the place, and [be] unmanageable for me." Early in the treatment, Steve had strongly resisted interpretations involving issues such as displacement. Now, as a finding from his own process of self-inquiry, Steve was able to reflect upon and describe a certain kind of overwhelming experience in his everyday life as the painful result of maladaptive displacement.

He was able to conceptualize rather precisely what he felt had been helpful to him in the analytic treatment, for him a matter of process more than particular content or issues. This came up after one of his regular weekend visits with his new foster-family. Steve had been working out at a health club in their community, and Steve struck up a conversation with a young adult he had met there while working out. Steve told him that he was in the process of leaving a residential facility, where he had also been in therapy. The somewhat older man responded by saying, "Oh, therapy doesn't do anything while you're just a teenager." Steve didn't argue with him, but in session he stated that he thought his acquaintance had absolutely no conception or understanding of what therapy had been like for him. At first I responded somewhat defensively to his acquaintance's criticism of therapy by externalizing, observing that the objections reminded me of some of the older or classical ideas about how difficult it was to "do" psychotherapy or analysis with adolescents. I also wondered whether this fellow might have had a negative experience with therapy when he was younger. Then, turning to us, I said that instead of focussing upon his friend, I was more interested in hearing Steve's thoughts about what it was about therapy, or our work together, that he felt had been most helpful to him. He responded succinctly, "You've not been someone telling me what I think, or more, what I feel. It's been a *conversation*." This statement affirmed Steve's appreciation of the analytic process as a conversation, an interactive model as distinguished from a regressive monologue (Freud, 1926/1959; Gill, 1994; Lipton, 1977).

During the final days of Steve's stay at the school, he expressed a desire for me to accompany him on a couple of activities outside the session room. He very strongly wanted me to go with him to the university field house to watch him train and see his acquaintances there. He also wanted me to be with him while he said good-bye to the cleaning and kitchen staff at the school. Both of these instances of going outside the office, as termination gestures, could be viewed as enactments and deviations from the analytic frame. Occurring within the context of a total residential treatment milieu, however, the deviations could be examined and contribute new awareness about the closing phase of the treatment. In both situations, what he seemed to want was for me to witness his growing ability to empathically relate to a wide range of people outside of our immediate treatment setting. For example, it became clear at the field house that a number of the adults greatly admired Steve's weight-lifting ability and spent considerable time talking with him during their workout periods. For Steve's part, he demonstrated that he had been able to develop a reserved, yet friendly and poised way of relating to these acquaintances. In one potentially conflictual situation, two adults whom he had known for awhile, a man and a woman, presented him with decidedly different views about what they thought were the best lifting techniques for him. The woman was a body fitness trainer, while the man was a power lifter. It was touching to watch him listen politely and attentively to the views of each, and then to come calmly to his own decision based upon his own goals, which happened to be more in line with the woman's suggestions. The encounter seemed to be an example of Steve's psychological growth with regard to being able to successfully maneuver through the potential conflict of triangular relationships.

In another session, as we approached the very end of termination, Steve again began talking with nostalgia about all of the staff members and students who had been important to him during his years at the school. Suddenly, he became very quiet and, while looking at me, murmured, "Sweet. . . . " "Sweet?" I asked. "Yes," he replied, "like chocolate." With that, he returned to the theme of *Forrest Gump* which had emerged during an earlier phase of treatment. At that time, Steve had referred to the character Bubba as a metaphor for his friendly feelings with me. In this session, however, Steve launched into a dramatic oration of other parts of the movie, recapturing the real actor's performance to a degree that was truly stunning to me. At first, I was so amazed at his superb acting skill that I found myself somewhat in awe of his natural talent for acting, and I initially began to think of the process at the moment as once again providing him with the attuned admiration that he so often seemed to need in our relationship. But as I listened more carefully to the specifics of what he emphasized in his performance to me, I realized that there was another way of looking at what he was doing. I remembered that some of the major themes of *Forrest Gump* included the difficulties of the lives of the socially marginal and the issue of whether life is simply a matter of fate, or whether it also essentially involves the choices made. Perhaps even more fundamentally, the movie was concerned with how one human being, while coping with significant physical and cognitive impairments, managed a number of separations, losses, and endings in his important caretaking and love relationships.

"Chocolate, sweet cho-co-late," Steve repeated. I remembered that the first reference to chocolate occurred at the beginning of the movie, as Forrest sat with a box of chocolates and recalled that his mother had once told him, "Life is like a box of chocolates, you never know what you're gonna get." Of course, by the end of the movie, Forrest realized that while we may not know ahead of time what we will get, it is not all simply a matter of fate. For Steve also, there had been a realization that beyond the fact of his early traumatic experiences, he could begin to take the direction of his life into his own hands. The second major focus of Steve's performance was upon Forrest's declaration, "I love you." In the movie, this phrase, delivered in Forrest's moving, humble manner, occurred in two instances. The first time, he expressed it to his childhood sweetheart and later bride, "I can't help it, I love you." In the second instance, at the very end of the movie, it is expressed within the context of the father-son relationship, where Forrest says goodbye to his son, a leaving, by reminding the son of his feelings of devotion, "I want to tell you I love you." This was perhaps a metaphoric expression of one aspect of Steve's experience with me and the analysis as he surveyed our years together, the expression of a positively valanced, eroticized transference which had been both facilitating and restorative (Lachmann, 1994).

In later sessions during that last week, Steve continued to express feelings of identification with my therapeutic functions, repeating his earlier wish that some day, after graduating from college, he could return to the school and work as a counselor with children. He talked with some regret about having to leave the school, that in all his years the school was "the only home I ever really had." Beyond the metaphoric expressions of affectionate feelings given in his Forrest Gump performance, Steve was able at the very end to be even more direct. "I'll miss you . . . you'll have a lot of time to fill up now," he said. "You're right," I replied, "I'll miss you, too. Over the years, we've had such times together." He wondered about the details of my everyday life at home and in my neighborhood, when I wasn't working. Anticipating coming to see me away from the school in a month, he became more and more curious about what my private office looked like. Getting ready to leave our last analytic session, Steve quietly said, "We won't be apart too long. I'm going to make sure to see you. I'll miss you."

Considerations on the Closing Phase

With regard to the issue of termination in child and adolescent analytic treatment, Novick (1990) has pointed out that there is a variable capacity to meet the traditional conditions for adult termination. Novick has proposed a blend of the classical model, with its focus on the past, with a forward looking view of what could be new for the patient. Regarding the latter, the analyst needs to assess the degree to which there has been a restoration to the path of "progressive development," as evidenced by the strength of non-regressive forces in the youth's relationship with parents, the analyst, and with him- or herself. In addition, Novick looked for some identification with and internalization of the analyst's inquiring functions, resulting in a degree of self-analytic capacity. Finally, he looked for a shift in the patient's source of self-esteem and pleasure, from grandiose fantasy toward realistic achievements. Despite the seeming shift forward to the concept of developmental progression as the most reliable and overarching indicator for termination, the notion of the resolution of oedipal issues as a primary termination phase goal for children and adolescents persists in other reports on adolescent analysis (Parsons, 1990; Schmukler, 1990). It is, of course, more likely the case that these are not exclusionary issues. For example, in Steve's case the progressive restoration was probably enabled by the awareness of oedipal issues, but this growth was also facilitated by attention to earlier preoedipal factors related to issues of early development, such as his needs for attachment, mirroring, holding, benevolent object relations, the capacity to bear and contain affect, and the satisfaction of his longing for an exclusive relationship. In other words, the earlier and oedipal issues are not mutually exclusive. In fact, when oedipal issues came to the forefront in treatment, as they often did in this presentation, they were superimposed on the earlier difficulties and took on a texture that combined the two developmental perspectives. In other words, Steve's oedipal issues were strongly colored by the earlier deficits and vulnerabilities affecting the structure and functioning of his personality.

Looking at the closing phase of this analytic treatment, Steve demonstrated a number of achievements which can be conceptualized in terms of some of the termination criteria suggested by Novick. With regard to oedipal issues, during the course of treatment Steve had few recollections of early triadic interactions with his mother and father. However, beneath his avowed hatred for the mother there appeared intense preoedipal needs for maternal mirroring, along with wishes for attunement and the gratification of primary needs. These wishes seem to have been displaced to his father, who turned out to be unable to function as a part of Steve's world. The transference of these wishes to me, wishes for me to be a gratifying figure in Steve's world, appeared graphically in Steve's fantasy of me joining him at his Rock and Roll Club complex, where I shared with him the experience of his getting all of his primary needs adequately fulfilled. During the termination phase, his wish for me to be with him at the university field house could be seen as another display of his wish for me to be a part of his world, although it seemed to be a more realistic one. Overall, there was a movement away from a heavy reliance upon me for psychic gratification, toward a growing sense of initiative and ability to satisfy his own emotional and real life needs, as well as an enhanced ability for self-inquiry. Indeed, his active participation in the realization of a move to a community-based, foster-family living situation seemed to represent a significant restoration to the path of progressive development and a decisive new step into the real world. Information received 1 year after termination seemed to confirm the resumption of progressive growth, indicating that Steve was functioning well within his foster-family, as well as in his ability to cope with the academic and social demands of attending public high school and maintaining part-time employment in his community.

Seen from another perspective, as this commentary has noted earlier, Steve's oedipal experience did not seem to be transferred to separate external objects in a triadic manner. Rather, in his present life the oedipal conflict often appeared to be transferred to single primary objects, or adult caretaking persons. In particular, Steve was enraged by his perception of his caretakers' thoughts or interests which he interpreted as distracting the caretaker from him, even when they were only minimally divergent from his own. Those ideas and thoughts were often experienced as an intrusive third person in the oedipal triangle. Over time, Steve achieved a greater ability to tolerate perspectives different from his own, as well as an acknowledgement of the reality that there is such a thing as a basic element of triangulation in object relations. These achievements seemed to be associated with a diminished sense of grandiosity and entitlement, in both his relations with others and his athletic strivings.

The transference neurosis in this analysis can also perhaps be understood from a relational and environmental perspective. There tended to be an ongoing negative transference to the residential treatment milieu as the bad parent. In his past, Steve had never had anyone to step in on his behalf to deal with the bad parent; he had been left alone to deal with the bad object. Further, he felt that he didn't have the resources to do anything about that. So in the treatment setting, he was able to begin fighting against the perceived bad objects in the residential environment, while also having me to address both the malignant objects' bad behaviors and his own. In the ongoing transference to me, I was viewed and experienced both as nurturing and also as having intervening power. Steve's experiences with bad objects came to have a different outcome. In the individual treatment setting, Steve could say, "Isn't that wrong?" and get validation, as well as some modulation of his own retaliatory, aggressive feelings. He was able to begin reliving his childhood experiences, but with a crucial difference. In treatment, he had been able to add a good object to the old equation.

CONCLUSION

This paper presented a commentary on the analytic treatment of a depressed, highly agitated, and often rageful adolescent boy in residential care. Given the boy's ongoing experiences of desperation, a constructivist analytic treatment perspective seems to have helped to foster his psychological growth and sense of optimism about the future. It was an approach which at varying times focussed upon the discussion, symbolization, and enactment of massive feelings of loss, misunderstanding, disappointment, and rage. From this persistent struggle in the face of despair, within a vibrant sense of mutual engagement, emerged a growing sense of hopefulness, wishes for intimate human connection, and special feelings of attachment within the context of the here-and-now therapist-patient interactions. Although the boy's daily life in residential care was often marked by verbally explosive episodes, over time they became diminished both in duration and intensity. In addition, he became increasingly able to work with his therapist and other staff members at the school to build a life comprised of "new experiences," a life which was in striking contrast to the traumatic world of his disappointing past.

REFERENCES

Aichhorn, A. (1925/1965). *Wayward Youth*. New York: The Viking Press.

Aichhorn, A. (1964). *Delinquency and Child Guidance: Selected Papers*. (Eds. O. Fleischmann, P. Kramer, and H. Ross). New York: International Universities Press (Menninger Clinic Monograph Series No. 15).

Altman, N. (1997). The case of Ronald. Oedipal issues in the treatment of a seven-year-old boy. *Psychoanalytic Dialogues*, 7 (6), 725-739.

Bettelheim, B. (1950). *Love Is Not Enough*. New York: Free Press.

Bettelheim, B. (1955). *Truants from Life*. New York: Free Press.

Bettelheim, B. (1967). *The Empty Fortress.* New York: Free Press.

Bettelheim, B. (1974). *A Home for the Heart.* New York: Alfred A. Knopf.

Bleiberg, E. (1987). Stages in the treatment of narcissistic children and adolescents. *Bulletin of the Menninger Clinic, 51* (3), 296-313.

Borowitz, G. H. (1970). The therapeutic utilization of emotions and attitudes evoked in the caretakers of disturbed children. *British Journal of Medical Psychology, 43,* 129-139.

Ekstein, R., Wallerstein, J. S., & Mandelbaum (1992). Countertransference in the residential treatment of children. In J. R. Brandell (Ed.), *Countertransference in Psychotherapy with Children and Adolescents* (pp. 59-87). Northvale, NJ: Jason Aronson, Inc.

Freud, A. (1930/1973). Four lectures on psychoanalysis for teachers and parents. In *The Writings of Anna Freud,* Vol. 1, 73-133. New York: International Universities Press.

Freud, A. (1941-45/1973). Monthly reports to the foster parents' plan for war children, Inc., New York. In *The Writings of Anna Freud,* Vol. 3, 3-540. New York: International Universities Press.

Freud, A., & Burlingham, D. (1944/1973). Infants without families: The case for and against residential nurseries. In *The Writings of Anna Freud,* Vol. 3, 543-664. New York: International Universities Press.

Freud, S. (1926). The question of lay analysis. *Standard Edition,* 20: 177-250. London: Hogarth Press, 1959.

Ghent, E. (1992). Paradox and process. *Psychoanalytic Dialogues, 2* (2), 135-159.

Ghent, E. (1995). Interaction in the psychoanalytic situation. *Psychoanalytic Dialogues, 5* (3), 479-491.

Gill, M. M. (1993). One-person and two-person perspectives: Freud's "Observations on transference love." In S. Person, A. Hagelin, and P. Fonagy (Eds.), *On Freud's "Observations on Transference Love"* (pp. 114-129). New Haven, CT, and London: Yale University Press.

Gill, M. M. (1994). *Psychoanalysis in Transition.* Hillsdale, NJ: The Analytic Press.

Heller, P. (Ed.). (1992). *Anna Freud's Letters to Eva Rosenfeld.* Madison, CT: International Universities Press.

Hoffman, I. Z. (1991). Discussion: Toward a social-constructivist view of the psychoanalytic situation. *Psychoanalytic Dialogues, 1* (1), 74-105.

Hoffman, I. Z. (1994). Dialectical thinking and therapeutic action in the psychoanalytic process. *Psychoanalytic Quarterly, 63* (2), 187-218.

Hoffman, I. Z. (in press). *Ritual and Spontaneity in the Psychoanalytic Process: A Dialectical-Constructivist View.* Hillsdale, NJ: The Analytic Press.

Klein, G, (1969). Freud's two theories of sexuality. In M. M. Gill & P. Holzman (Eds.), *Psychology versus Metapsychology Psychological Issues,* Monograph 36 (pp. 14-70). New York: International Universities Press.

Lachmann, F. M. (1994). How can I eroticize thee? Let me count the ways. *Psychoanalytic Inquiry, 14* (4), 604-621.

Levy, E. Z. (1967). The importance of the children's needs in residential treatment. *Bulletin of the Menninger Clinic, 31* (1), 18-31.

Lipton, S. D. (1977). The advantages of Freud's techniques as shown in his analysis of the rat man. *International Journal of Psychoanalysis, 58* (3), 255-273.

Mitchell, S. A. (1993). *Hope and Dread in Psychoanalysis.* New York: Basic Books.

Mitchell, S. A. (1997). *Influence and Autonomy in Psychoanalysis.* Hillsdale, NJ: The Analytic Press.

Neubauer, P. (1993). Playing: Technical implications. In A. J. Solnit, D. J. Cohen, & P. B. Neubauer (Eds.), *The Many Meanings of Play* (pp. 44-53). New Haven, CT: Yale University Press.

Novick, J. (1990). Comments on termination in child, adolescent and adult analysis. *Psychoanalytic Study of the Child, 45,* 419-436.

Parsons, M. (1990). Some issues affecting termination. *Psychoanalytic Study of the Child, 45,* 437-458.

Phillips, A. (1997). Making it new enough. Commentary on paper by Altman. *Psychoanalytic Dialogues, 7* (6), 741-752.

Pizer, S. A. (1992). The negotiation of paradox in the analytic process. *Psychoanalytic Dialogues, 2* (2).

Pizer, S. A. (1996). Negotiating Potential Space. Illusion, Play, Metaphor, and the Subjunctive. *Psychoanalytic Dialogues, 6* (5), 689-712.

Price, A. (1994). Effects of maternal deprivation on the capacity to play: A Winnicottian perspective on work with inner-city children. *Psychoanalytic Psychology, 11* (3), 341-355.

Redl, F., & Wineman, D. (1951). *Children Who Hate.* Glencoe, IL: The Free Press.

Redl, F., & Wineman, D. (1952). *Controls from Within.* Glencoe, IL: The Free Press.

Rinsley, D. B. (1980). *Treatment of the Severely Disturbed Adolescent.* New York and London: Jason Aronson.

Schmukler, A. G. (1990). Termination in midadolescence. *Psychoanalytic Study of the Child, 45,* 459-474.

Slavin, J. H. (1994). On making rules: Toward a reformation of transference in psychoanalytic treatment. *Psychoanalytic Dialogues, (4)* 2, 253-274.

Spiegel, S. (1994). An alternative to dream interpretation with children. *Contemporary Psychoanalysis, 30* (2), 384-395.

Zaslow, S. L. (1988). Comments on "Confusion of Tongues." *Contemporary Psychoanalysis, 24* (2), 211-225.

Zimmerman, D. P. (1993). The little turtle's progress: A reconsideration of the short versus long-term residential treatment controversy. *Children and Youth Services Review, 15* (3), 219-243.

Zimmerman, D. P., & Cohler, B. J. (1998). From disciplinary control to benign milieu in children's residential treatment. *Therapeutic Communities, 19* (2), 123-147.